BECOMING A PARENT: 16 TRUTHS AND A LIE

REFLECTIONS OF A NEW MOM NAVIGATING POSTPARTUM

COLLEEN M. IMLER

Library of Congress Control Number: 2024903835

Book Cover and Illustrations © Mickey Shu-Ting Chan and Dani Marcel, 2024

Author Photo © Christopher Kelly, 2022

ISBN: 979-8-2183-6122-8

ISNB: 979-8-2183-6123-5 (ebook)

❀ Created with Vellum

November 7, 2019
(Three weeks, five days)

Hi! I just found out you exist today! It has been a whirlwind of a day — woke up at 4 a.m. … I guess that is an omen of all the lack of sleep you'll "gift" me! I think I'm still in shock — it doesn't seem real yet. I hope I can step up to the plate and give you everything you need. Purpose, safety, love, passion, and kindness. I realize our lives are now changed forever and I can't wait to meet you and watch this new adventure unfold. We love you already.

— Colleen (aka Mom)

To the one who made me a mom, you teach me more than any classroom has. You give me strength, help me find my voice and I love witnessing the world through your eyes.

I am forever grateful for you, my sweet Adeline.

CONTENTS

INTRODUCTION

*Owning our story and loving ourselves through that process
is the bravest thing we'll ever do.*
—Brené Brown

Congratulations, you (or someone you love) are pregnant! Yippie! Buckle your "adulting" seatbelts because the rest of your life is going to be a thrilling ride full of twists and turns, highs and lows, and bumps here and there, but hopefully you have a great partner and/or support system along with you for the ride.

Everyone's journey of parenthood is different. Try not to be envious of others' experiences, but instead work every day to embrace your own. You are meant to learn different lessons in life than your friends, coworkers, and family members. Choose your own path and let's keep the conversation going. You are not alone.

This book takes you through a lot of my personal journey. Not my sister-in-law's, not my husband's, not my best friend's—mine. My journey as a woman, as a wife, and as a new mother. My hope is that something will resonate with you and provide comfort, courage, or empowerment to keep you moving forward, even in the hardest of times.

The journey to becoming a parent (usually) starts when you and your partner make the decision to try—whether you try to conceive the old-fashioned way, try by injecting hormones, try by applying for adoption, etc. Some endure months (and some years) trying to get pregnant and then, suddenly, your efforts are successful. You are then blessed with more time—forty-plus weeks—to prepare for this life change while nurturing and growing a human inside of you. I'll be honest, that final month can feel like a full year—and not in the way you'd want it to.

There's something magical about the due date month that makes you feel like you're close to the finish line. The excitement sparks—and for a lot of people, it burns too hot. Burns them out. In technical terms, you *are* close to the extraordinary finish line that is giving birth, but man does that last month drag out. It grinds you down. When you are mentally, emotionally, and physically "done," every day that goes by without a newborn baby in your arms can crush your spirit.

It did for me anyway.

That's one of the biggest reasons I wrote this book: Because pregnancy can be so much more complicated than the books will tell you. Because you deserve to hear the real, unvarnished details, not just skim through airbrushed Instagram photos.

After I gave birth to my daughter, I asked some of my

friends why no one had told me how hard things could really be. Their answer? "Well . . . then people wouldn't have kids."

Clearly, that's not totally true. After all, plenty of people have multiple children, even knowing what it was like the first time. But it still speaks to a real silence in our culture around the difficulties of pregnancy and having children. A silence that only worsens the huge lack of support for mothers and new parents in many countries and leads a lot of women to struggle more than they need to, unable to get the help or *real* information that they need.

So, I'm here to help you on your journey—to help you get the information you need.

I'm here to help you prepare for and take care of yourself during one of the most momentous, painful, tedious, amazing times of your life: bringing a child into this world.

And just as importantly, I'm here to help you take care of yourself afterward.

SECTION ONE

LEADING UP TO THE BIG DAY

TRUTH #1

TIME DOESN'T FOLLOW THE RULES WHEN YOU'RE PREGNANT (OR A NEW PARENT)

Time is free, but it's priceless. You can't own it, but you can use it. You can't keep it, but you can spend it. Once you've lost it, you can never get it back.
—Harvey MacKay

THE FIRST YEAR with my baby was both the longest and the fastest year of my life. A literal oxymoron. I don't understand how time can move so slowly in those first few weeks, even when the baby's development and month-to-month milestones occur at lightspeed.

In my opinion, time is a thief.

Let's start by setting some realistic expectations for your pregnancy timeline (and that wondrous final month) that some pregnancy books might not dive into.

For the majority of those who give birth it's not anywhere near how it is portrayed in the movies. Plus, the screenwriters don't even account for timing of recovery and postpartum in the mix. Same goes for those in your tribe who have also had the experience of giving birth. Why? Probably because it's not pretty or glamorous. It's challenging and can completely drain your energy. It's not a one-size-fits-all experience. All this said, we need to talk about it. We are doing a disservice to ourselves and future new parents by keeping the rough side of becoming a parent under lock and key. That's why I decided to put it all on the table.

YOUR PREGNANCY TIMELINE

Yes, the first trimester is exciting. You are sharing the news with loved ones and experiencing new sensations and feelings. You might have more or less time in the first trimester —from your perspective, that is—depending on how and when you found out about your pregnancy. Enjoy the time you do have! Lean into the buzz of excitement and appreciate whatever freedoms you cherish the most, because a lot of them are going to take a break for somewhere between eight months and eighteen years.

The second trimester is the best because typically you physically feel pretty good and those rough first trimester symptoms have subsided. Your bump is starting to "show" and you are exploring the joy of maternity clothes. You are also to the point where your ultrasounds and bloodwork have given you more knowledge about your baby, including any health or development risks. For many, this point of the pregnancy either provides great peace of mind or constant stress.

The third trimester starts off decent, but as you get closer and closer to that mighty due date, your body is rapidly changing to accommodate a quickly growing baby. Did you know that most of the weight for you and the baby is packed on in the final two months? This is also when you might start feeling anxious about what is to come. Tour the hospital so you know where to park and check in, attend birthing classes, and pack the hospital bag, because it "could happen any moment now."

Don't let the trimesters fool you. Some symptoms you experience in the first several weeks can last the entire duration of your pregnancy, and other times you'll have "symptom roulette" and experience something different each week. Some people have very positive pregnancy experiences, and others not so much. Remember, each person (and pregnancy) is different.

By forty weeks, your body is basically carrying a watermelon, and in my case, I enjoyed the humid heat of a New Jersey summer. I had to buy sandals with Velcro adjustable straps to accommodate my very swollen feet, basically my go-to footwear for the last month. Otherwise, I would have been right out of a country song: barefoot and pregnant. But don't worry, the uncomfortable (very pregnant) feeling is temporary. And as we all know, forty weeks is right about when things get *really* interesting.

WAITING, WAITING, WAITING

Our due date—that forty-week mark, that beautiful, theoretical finish line—was July 18, 2020. Four months into COVID and nine months into pregnancy.

Funnily enough, we had close friends who were due on July 14. We were both expecting (and joking) that we would go into labor and welcome our babies into the world at the same time.

But of course, pregnancy never follows the rules. My friend went into labor ten days earlier than she anticipated, on July 4, and I was induced and welcomed our baby ten days after I had hoped to go into labor, on July 28.

That wait was so suspenseful. Really, life is surreal every day during the due date month. It makes you feel like it could happen at any moment. All the articles on the websites say, "Pack your hospital bag so you're prepared at thirty-five weeks." But really, that just makes the other five (or in my case, seven) weeks that much more mentally and physically draining.

Don't get me wrong, it's great to be prepared, and I'm glad that I was very meticulous about our hospital bag—especially with COVID-19 restrictions forcing us to plan with many unanswered questions about what the hospital experience would really be like. But it was also very, very stressful.

Every day, I felt like I was about to go into labor. As a first-time mom, you just don't know what to expect. Everything and anything feels like it could be a sign of labor. I remember feeling wet, and I wasn't sure if my water was breaking slowly (because, of course, I searched online and found it's possible to slowly leak) or if I was just, you know, wet. I didn't know what a true labor contraction felt like, so every time I had a surge or Braxton-Hicks, I thought to myself, "Oh my god, this is it!" and was overcome with excitement and nervousness. That was easy to manage for maybe the first week. But after that, it gets *old* fast.

It's true what they say, actually: you'll know when it's legit labor. But it's one thing for people to say that and a very different thing to actually believe it, especially when so many new things are happening to your body all the time!

"IT'S TIME" (NOT)

For some strange reason, I always thought I was going to go into labor in the middle of the night. You know the drill: wake up at 3:00 a.m. with surging pains, proceed to wake my husband, and tell him, "It's time." Gather our things, call our parents in the middle of the night, and head to the hospital. A story straight out of a medical drama.

Spoiler alert: that's not how it happened.

As we made it halfway through the third trimester, of course, we made sure that we would be ready. (Or, at least, "ready.") At one point, I kept having so many episodes of Braxton-Hicks, we just packed the car, so it was ready. But weeks went by and still no baby.

I'm not going to lie—it was hard. Every morning, especially those last two to three weeks, I'd wake up and just cry because the baby hadn't arrived, and I had to push through yet another day of waiting.

I worked from home up until my due date, and that week, I swore I was going to go into labor. I just had a *feeling*. I even told my team, "Hey, I think I'm going to go into labor early, so everything is set and prepared for the transition ahead of my maternity leave."

Finally, my last day of work came, and still, no baby.

Working up to my due date kept my mind somewhat distracted, which was good, but my body was still exhausted. Most days, I would nap during my lunch break. Sometimes, I would even fall asleep and not wake up in time for a meeting. I was hot and miserable, hungry all the time, and alone in the house until my husband got home from work. And so, time dragged on.

Once I was officially on maternity leave, I was literally just waiting. Waiting, waiting, waiting—and I am now very self-aware of the fact that I do not have the most patience. The unknowing and constant waiting broke me down, mentally. I wanted the baby to be born simply because I didn't *want* to be pregnant anymore. Selfish, but true. My feet were swollen, I had high blood pressure, I was uncomfortable, and it was difficult to move. My "exercise" each day was to walk down to my mailbox and back. My hormones were raging, I cried every day, and at one point I literally said out loud to my mom, "This baby is never coming."

Which sounds super silly in hindsight. Of course the baby was coming, that's how babies work. But at the moment, I truly didn't think it was ever going to happen. I'd be that wild news story of a woman at forty-four weeks and still pregnant. Of course, this is a comical thought now since my midwives would never have let me go past forty-two weeks.

I tried to enjoy my last ten days of "freedom." Most of the advice I got was to either sleep or watch TV "while I still could." I didn't understand it. I just wanted my baby on the outside and not the inside. God, what I would give to travel back in time and tell myself to breathe, to stop worrying, that the baby will be healthy and happy, and to relax and just soak up those last moments. My anxiety was wasting my energy, and I was going to need every ounce for the labor, delivery, and postpartum that was heading my way.

I took pregnancy-status photos every couple of weeks during the nine months, more often toward the end. For my "forty week" and due date, I remember getting all dressed up —hair, makeup, I put on an actual dress. Not only was this a bizarre change of habit during the pandemic, but anyone who knows me understands I am not one to voluntarily put on a dress. But I was attempting to lift my spirits and enjoy the day—and wishing with all my might for the baby to come.

Did you know only 5 percent of birthdays occur on the due date, 73 percent occur before the due date, and 22 percent after? It's fascinating and makes me question why we so often talk about the due date as the end all, be all (literally!).

When it got to week forty-one, my husband asked if I wanted to take another weekly photo. I remember feeling hopeless, angry even. I didn't want to celebrate being pregnant still. We had been trying everything—well, mostly everything—to encourage this little one to make their grand entrance into the world, with no luck. I told him, "No, I'll be taking my forty-one-week photo in the hospital."

And gosh dang it, I sure did! At forty-one weeks and two days, I went to my routine checkup with the midwives. This was after taking a two-mile walk that morning with my mom in our local state park. When they checked my vitals, they said my blood pressure was too elevated, and since I was past my due date, they wanted me to check into the hospital for an induction.

Like it or not, this was it. My "it's time" moment.

The next seventy-two hours would feel like seven days, and the first several weeks of being home with the baby would slowly crawl by.

But that didn't matter in the end—my baby had finally arrived.

TRUTH #2

YOU ARE NOT IN THE DRIVER'S SEAT

Change is the only constant in life. One's ability to adapt to those changes will determine your success in life.
—Benjamin Franklin

During my pregnancy journey, one of the best pieces of advice was to listen to an array of labor and delivery stories. This is the same advice I pass on to expectant moms in my life—and part of the inspiration for this book. Talking to friends and family, listening to podcasts, reading books, and of course, consulting with your midwife or doctor about a birthing plan.

I remember confidently sharing with my midwife that, "I didn't really have a plan." I wanted to go with the flow and be flexible. Ultimately, I knew that any plan I made wouldn't matter in the end. I wasn't in control. The midwives seemed to extend a sigh of relief, agreeing the birth would be on the baby's terms and my "no plan" plan could very well be the best option for me.

In my professional life, I always err on the side of caution, have backup plans, think through scenarios that could happen, etc. So, that's obviously how I imagined handling my own labor and delivery: go with the flow but prepare myself for all the options. I wanted to be educated on the different types of delivery choices and any possible necessary actions the midwife and delivery nurses might have to take based on the health and safety of me or my baby.

In reality—and a tough truth to swallow—my "no plan" plan was great, but only up until I was alone and masked sitting in a patient room, being told I needed to drive to the hospital, check in, and be induced.

I broke down. I cried because I had successfully avoided induced labor for the last four weeks by managing my high blood pressure after it was flagged to me. I cried because I wasn't ready—and I thought my baby wasn't ready. If my baby was ready to enter the world, they would rev up the engine and start the process.

I cried because, in that moment, I realized I failed through all the attempts to "naturally induce" myself into labor. All the walking, drinking tea, having sex, bouncing on a ball, exercising, eating pineapple, stimulating nipples, eating spicy foods . . . all for nothing. I cried because I felt alone, anxious, and scared even though I had been trying to convince myself for months that I was okay only having one support person with me due to COVID and hospital restrictions.

I still wanted my mom to be there. Every time I had an appointment in the months leading up to delivery, I'd ask if the hospital had adjusted their policy at all. No dice. It was official: having my mom in the room was off the table.

I cried because the midwife telling me this daunting news

was completely new to the practice, and well, you never know . . . she could be wrong! But unfortunately, she wasn't wrong. She even got a second opinion from another midwife on duty because of how upset I was. She tried to calm me down and even let me sit in a quiet space for some time so that she could retake my blood pressure. But I was a lost cause. My emotions, hormones, and body were giving up. In my mind, I had to admit defeat. It was time.

We checked ourselves into the hospital, after getting lost on the grounds and walking the entire perimeter of the building looking for the main entrance. Don't even get me started. Thanks to COVID, there were no hospital tours beforehand, and we both were experiencing extra high levels of stress and anxiety, so we clearly were not thinking straight. Mindlessly searching for the entrance.

THE INDUCTION

An induction is when your healthcare provider needs to administer medicine or use other inducing methods to help jumpstart your labor. Many times, this happens if you or your baby's health is at risk or if you're past your due date. Inducing labor is typically only performed for medical reasons to help keep Mom and baby healthy. For me, it was because of high blood pressure, which can be very dangerous when it comes to giving birth.

My induction started around 5:00 p.m. on Monday, July 27, and we welcomed our daughter at 7:48 p.m. on Tuesday, July 28. Nearly twenty-seven hours from start to finish.

They started by dilating my cervix with the help of an instrument called a foley bulb—a thin tube with a balloon at the end that gets inserted into the vagina to widen the cervix. The balloon is slowly inflated with saline solution, putting pressure on the cervix to promote dilation and contractions. This is left in place until the cervix is officially three centimeters dilated. Remember, the goal is ten centimeters for delivery, so progression helped to get nearly a third of the way there. This process took twelve very uncomfortable hours.

And that, my friends, was the first of many terrible sleepless nights.

It didn't help that the entire day was filled with anxiety, frustration, and tears. I was hooked up to multiple machines, still *very* pregnant and uncomfortable, lying in a cold hospital room where the air conditioner was drumming very loudly, and no peace would be had that night. Any moment where I was able to drift off to sleep, I was soon visited by the labor nurses who did their jobs well, checking my vitals and adjusting my monitors throughout the night.

I was so excited when 5:00 a.m. arrived, because I knew I was going to get the stupid balloon out. That ended up coming an hour later, but nonetheless I was able to get out of bed, eat some breakfast, take a shower, and ultimately continue to wait. While my cervix was dilated to three centimeters now, nothing else was happening. We had to continue onward to the next phase of my induction.

After my shower but before that next phase, I *finally* took my forty-one-plus-week bump photo. The last evidence of my pregnant, non-parent self. In the hospital, just like I'd declared. Looking back, this was a huge milestone. If I had any tears left at that point in time, I probably would have cried.

For the next phase, they started me on Pitocin, a synthetic version of oxytocin given through an IV, which helps stimulate the uterus muscles and causes contractions to push the baby through the laboring process. It was during that first hour that I finally understood what people meant when they told me, "Oh you'll know if it's a *real* contraction," and not Braxton-Hicks, which is when your abdomen tightens in waves to help prepare your uterus for birth. The descriptions I've heard people say about contractions are spot on. Cramps that intensify, creating a tight sensation that takes over your entire uterus and abdominal area. It's very much like a roller coaster, gradually becoming more intense and then descending back down to resting, and then repeating itself over a timed cadence. The timing of intervals helps you gauge how close you are to the real finish line: bringing the baby into the world.

My contractions started off slow and were manageable, but as most birthing stories go, it got worse as the hours dragged on. I don't really remember much of it to be honest, but once it started getting difficult to manage, I no longer wanted to lie down. I stood up and bent over a foot stool on my hands and knees. I learned another part of my "non-plan" birth plan was that I wanted the satisfaction of getting through labor without an epidural. I listened to audiobooks, I read laboring techniques, I packed essential oils, printed mantras on paper, practiced massages, and planned to focus on my breathing. That said, I was never 100 percent against getting an epidural, I just wanted to accomplish giving birth without it. After all, women used to give birth in grassy fields. Surely, I could manage.

For a short time, I labored in a large birthing tub, which was nice and took pressure off my body. At this point, my midwife checked my cervix and declared I was still only six centimeters dilated. I remember asking her in desperation how much longer it would be, with a pleading tone in my voice. She looked me in the eyes and said, "There is no way to know. It could be thirty minutes, or it could be four hours."

I was still exhausted from the previous day, having no decent rest, and bearing through the uncomfortable experience of induction. I was trying to muster up the strength to push through the pain with each rolling contraction, but I was anxious, and my body just didn't have the energy that I hoped it would have to get through it. I cried at my own defeat and nodded to my midwife to call the anesthesiologist to administer the epidural.

My choice to accept help and receive the epidural was the best decision I made during that entire forty-eight hours. My husband, Kyle, said I was like a different person after getting it. I relaxed, even smiled, and was able to somewhat prepare for the birth of our baby. In hindsight, I'm especially relieved I got the epidural, as the delivery included some minor complications that I am glad I was essentially numb from the waist down for.

Around 6:00 p.m. I was finally nine centimeters dilated, and we decided to wait one more hour before I officially started pushing. The moment was surreal, one last hour of just the two of us and the baby tucked safely inside. As we approached 7:00 p.m., I started to feel a heavy sense of pressure, which was that "ready to push" concept I had heard so many times while listening to birthing stories.

Then the real work began. I started to push and did that for about thirty-five minutes. Pushing was a lot harder than I thought it was going to be. Oddly, everything that I had read and practiced was the opposite of what they told me to do in the delivery room. I read advice on deep breathing, and instead they told me to hold my breath. I also clearly remember them advising me to not scream or yell, since it would do nothing except make my throat sore. At this point I was very thankful for the epidural. All this aside, I can only imagine what this entire labor and delivery experience was like for my husband, watching me go through it all and unable to do anything except be there as my "support person." I'm pretty sure I kept my eyes closed the whole time —not that I could really see anything anyway.

The baby's heart rate started to be compromised by the constant pushing and no real headway—literally. She was not making her way fully through the birth canal. My midwife made the decision to conduct an episiotomy: a surgical cut made at the opening of the vagina to help with difficult deliveries and prevent rupture of tissues. Episiotomies are not as common anymore, especially among midwives, but it's sometimes necessary based on the conditions of the mother and the baby. In addition to my episiotomy, I had multiple vaginal tears by the time it was done.

But finally, my baby was out.

This is when we finally discovered we had a daughter, and Kyle told me it was a girl. Her heart rate was a concern, so as soon as she was born, a team of neonatal nurses swarmed in to check her over. I remember my midwife crouched next to my bed and told me what had happened, what she had to do and that she was asking the surgeon to come help with recovery efforts. My newborn daughter was placed in my arms for what seemed like two seconds, and then she was taken to the nursery to be monitored for her heart. At this point, Kyle had the option to stay with me or go with our daughter. He looked at me, and without hesitation I told him to go. In hindsight, that was my first selfless "mom gut" decision.

THE AFTERMATH

I'm not going to sugarcoat this next part. The next forty-five minutes were god-awful. The surgeon came and started cleaning and stitching me back up. I was losing a lot of blood, and at one point there was a discussion among the surgeon and nurses whether I needed to relocate to the ER. I completely lost my mind at this point. I didn't have my baby, and I didn't have my husband. I was getting painfully stitched up in the most sensitive and private area of my body. There I was: spread eagle, bleeding after just giving birth, and getting my lady bits sewn back together after being ripped and cut. I don't even remember delivering the placenta, but obviously I know it happened.

I was getting very upset, crying a lot, and my anxiety was rushing over me. The surgeon and nurses were trying their best to calm me down. I don't know why, but to cope with the fear and the unknown, I started singing Broadway show songs. I'm talking smash hits from *Wicked*, *Hamilton*, *Frozen* . . . even some oldies from my high school theater days. The nurses got a chuckle out of it, and we soon started laughing and singing together as the surgeon did what he had to do.

I started to gain more feeling below my waist, my epidural was wearing off, but the surgeon still had more to do. Eventually Kyle came back into the delivery room, and he told me more about our daughter. She was doing well, and the nurses said they would bring her back to us once they felt she was ready. After I was officially stitched up, next came post-birth internal evaluations and removal of blood clots. This was literally the worst part since I had full feeling during it. I spiked a fever and my heart rate started to decline. I still didn't have my baby back in my arms. I knew I missed out on the "golden hour," known as the first hour after a baby is born that many mothers use as a bonding time for skin-to-skin with the umbilical cord still attached. I was even more exhausted than I was before. It was 10:00 p.m., and we were frantically trying to find a way to order food for me to eat, as I was very hungry.

That's when I had a panic attack, wishing I was back in the comfort of my own home and not in a sterile hospital room.

The point of sharing my labor and delivery story is not to scare you but to reinforce that you have very little control over what you are about to experience. It's okay if your birth plan goes off course—you are not alone. Remember that your feelings are valid, and you aren't doing anything wrong. If you are religious, this is likely the moment when you cry out, "Jesus, take the wheel!" Still, even today, I get envious of friends, family, coworkers who have a picture-perfect labor and delivery story. Sure, it was still tough for them, but they were able to hold their baby moments after, Dad cut the cord, the room echoed with celebration and immediately shared the joy with friends and family. That just wasn't the case for us.

I hate when people say, "Childbirth is tough, but it'll all be worth it in the end. It's all worth it when you have that baby in your arms." For me, it wasn't until Monday, June 14, 2021, forty-seven weeks after delivering my daughter, that I said out loud without hesitation, "It was all worth it." Worth the challenging labor, the less-than-ideal delivery, and the traumatic recovery that lasted months.

I love my child with every ounce of my being, and I couldn't imagine life without her, but I struggled with coming to terms with my experience for almost a full year afterward, until I was finally able to heal from postpartum depression and make amends with myself. And although my transition into motherhood was traumatic—and so were the attendant life lessons—I came out on the other side to my wonderful, smart, and kind little girl. A whole, tiny human being who was by then walking, babbling, and playing with her parents before bed. She was absolutely worth it.

TRUTH #3
THERAPY HAS A PLACE IN YOUR PREGNANCY TOOLKIT

Asking for help is a sign of strength, not a sign of weakness.
—Laurie A. Watkins

IF YOU DO a Google search on "what to pack in your hospital bag," you'll find thousands of articles and videos from influencers, media websites, brands, and other parenting organizations, all giving you their advice on what you'll need or want at your fingertips for those precious moments in the hospital when welcoming baby.

Sure, it's great to purchase your own delivery gown to help you be more comfortable, since you'll probably be wearing it for at least twenty-four hours, or pack a Bluetooth speaker to play your favorite tunes to help pass the time. So much thought, personalization, and time goes into what to pack for your sweet "getaway trip." Not to mention the extensive planning that goes into prepping the bag weeks in advance, ensuring you have everything organized, keeping it in an accessible spot—ready to grab and go at a moment's notice.

Unpopular opinion: ultimately, it doesn't *really* matter if you have your essential oils or diffusers to cope with the stress or printed affirmation cards to help you harness your inner maternal goddess. That baby will come one way or another. Instead of asking expectant mothers if their hospital bag is packed and ready, I suggest we discuss how they will cope, heal, and keep their mental health a priority once baby is born.

THE MENTAL HEALTH CONVERSATION

Ah, yes, the mental health conversation. A rare gem that—thanks to a global pandemic isolating and distancing friends and families for years, on top of fear of the unknown and the human need to protect loved ones—is *finally* becoming a less awkward conversation to have.

But why does it have such a negative stigma? Why do people perceive "seeing a therapist" as being broken, having a shameful illness, or something "too taboo" to discuss with others? Once upon a time I was that person. I thought, "If I go to a therapist, does that mean I'm crazy, weak, or a failure? What will others think? How will I get time off from work to go every other week? I obviously need to hide it."

Let me be clear—I am pro-therapy. Therapy changed my life. Sure, that's a dramatic statement, but I 100 percent believe it. The year 2019 was the toughest year of my life (at the time). I was getting physically ill from my inability to recognize and manage high stress and high anxiety. I had no idea what to do or what was wrong with me. After one morning, when a panic attack left me crying and shaking on my bathroom floor, I called my mom and admitted to her that I wasn't okay. She did what any caring mother would do in this type of situation: she told me to take a deep breath and that she was leaving in ten minutes to drive to my house and take me to get help.

I was examined thoroughly by my primary care provider. They did a range of bloodwork and medical tests. Everything came back normal. I was "healthy." Yet, I didn't feel healthy. I felt weak, my stomach was churning, I was very often experiencing what I like to call "nervous poo," and of course, the little voice in the back of my head kept telling me that this was not a good time to have a nervous breakdown. I had so much to handle at home and at work. The nurse practitioner looked at me and softly suggested that I should consider talking to a counselor. I was immediately embarrassed. I'd bet money that my face turned as red as a fire hydrant.

There I was, a young, intelligent, highly educated, driven woman, being told I have a mental health problem. I'll be honest, I was *not* open to the idea of a counselor at first. About a month later, after experiencing even more anxiety, I finally bit the bullet. I swallowed my pride and searched on PsychologyToday.com to find therapists in my area. That's when I stumbled on the bio of Lindsey, who had extensive professional experience with adults who encounter varying levels of depression and anxiety disorders. We had a match!

During the first two sessions, Lindsey went into detail about how she helps her clients, what her philosophies are, and her views on the necessity of having mental health conversations. She never showed signs of judgement and incorporated humor, enthusiasm, and positive energy into her sessions to help build a therapeutic alliance with her clients. According to Lindsey, everyone should be assigned a doctor and a therapist at birth. As a society, we typically put great emphasis on preventive care for our physical health, yet we don't do the same for our mental health. What she made me realize is that the two are intertwined. Your mental and physical abilities work together to either help you or work against you. At the time, mine were against me.

Can you imagine if children were taught from the beginning on how to identify and manage their physical and mental struggles? If they were encouraged to be open and talk about their struggles, and were reassured that what they were feeling was valid and not something to be ashamed of? It would inevitably have a domino effect on society. Creating mentally self-aware children who become mentally self-aware teenagers, and then transforming into mentally self-aware adults, and possibly, eventually, self-aware parents.

Since starting my therapy journey in June 2019, I am extremely proud of how far I've come. I am grateful for everything that took place that year. The events that transpired led me to face my mental struggles and not to be afraid to seek help. I've continued to practice what I've learned every day since. There is no doubt in my mind those events unfolded for a purpose: to prepare me for pregnancy, postpartum, motherhood (probably not the global pandemic part, but it certainly helped with that too), and beyond.

I'll let you in on a secret: you don't have to reach a breaking point, crying on the floor shaking, with your mom on the other end of the phone, before seeking help. There is no prescription needed to contact a counselor or therapist and just have a conversation. Talk about your mental health perception, struggles you face, how you currently cope with challenges, or what you hope to change about your habits. The world is changing. The pandemic set into motion progressive practices for a lot of industries. I think one of the biggest and very few blessings to come out of it is that mental health now has a seat at the table. Employers are speaking openly about it, family and friends are "checking in" more often, even insurance companies were waiving copays and insurance holder responsibilities for behavioral and mental health counseling services during the height of the pandemic.

Keep this in mind: adding therapy to your pregnancy toolkit doesn't automatically set you up to navigate postpartum with ease. I had all the knowledge, tools, and resources, and I still experienced Postpartum Mood and Anxiety Disorders (PMADs). I'm not ashamed of that. I'm also not alone. Almost one in five individuals struggle with this—including partners.

Mental health is something that you work through and practice every single day. You don't just recover and move on like you do with a broken bone after twelve weeks of physical therapy. Life will continue to throw you curveballs, and hormones will make you cry at midnight, but ultimately being open to the conversation and having a therapist just a text away gave me hope when I was feeling my lowest.

During my preparation for childbirth, I read books, talked to professionals, listened to podcasts, and took classes online. I often heard about the "baby blues"—feelings of sadness that you might experience the first few days after having a baby. Statistics show that four in five new parents, that is a whopping 80 percent, experience the baby blues. What causes such a high statistic? After delivery, the levels of hormones in your bloodstream, including estrogen and progesterone, suddenly decrease, which causes mood swings. For some, the hormones made by the thyroid gland may drop sharply, which can make you feel tired and depressed. They say the postpartum hormone drop is considered the single largest hormone change in the shortest amount of time for any human being, at any point in their life cycle. Tack this on to not getting adequate sleep or eating well, and it only adds to those negative feelings.

But here's the thing: as normal as they say it is to feel emotional highs and lows during that time, baby blues typically go away within one to two weeks after giving birth—no medical treatment needed. PMADs are a different story, and they're also the thing I *didn't* hear about, even though I had a pre-existing condition for them, a history of anxiety.

PMADS BY THE NUMBERS

Approximately 15 percent of all women will experience postpartum depression following the birth of a child. Up to 10 percent will experience depression or anxiety during pregnancy. When the mental health of the mother is compromised, it affects the entire family. And this isn't just siloed to the first six weeks of postpartum either. Symptoms can appear *any time* during pregnancy and the first twelve months after childbirth. While Postpartum Depression (PPD) is most talked about, there are actually several other forms of illness that you may experience, including Postpartum Anxiety (PPA), Postpartum Obsession and Compulsion Disorder (PPOCD), Postpartum Traumatic Stress Disorder (PPTSD), Bipolar Mood Disorder, and Postpartum Psychosis (PPP).

Let's explore what each of these PMADs might look like, so you know the warning signs.

- **Postpartum Anxiety.** Approximately 6 percent of pregnant women and 10 percent of postpartum women develop anxiety. Imagine feeling constant worry about your baby, your sleep and appetite are disturbed, you have racing thoughts, you are unable to sit still, and you have a steady, burning feeling that something bad will happen.

- **Postpartum Depression.** What's the difference from anxiety you might ask? With depression, you feel angry or irritable—it typically consists of constant crying and a sense of sadness. You lose interest in things you once loved or enjoyed, and you have an intense feeling of guilt, shame, or hopelessness. Fifteen percent of women experience significant depression after childbirth.

- **Postpartum Obsession and Compulsion Disorder.** This is the most misunderstood and misdiagnosed of the PMADs, with an estimated 3 to 5 percent of parents experiencing it. Imagine being repeatedly triggered by intrusive thoughts and mental images related to the baby that make it seem like it's in harm's way. This brings about actions that you do over and over again to try to avoid said harm. This can look like constantly cleaning, checking in constantly on the baby while sleeping, counting or reordering things like supplies or medicines, etc. It can be often viewed as hypervigilance in trying to protect the baby.

- **Postpartum Traumatic Stress Disorder.** About 9 percent of women experience this, often caused by real or perceived trauma during delivery or postpartum. Think emergency C-section, time in the NICU, or even experiencing previous trauma, such as domestic violence. This may look like intrusive reimagining of the traumatic experience though flashbacks or nightmares. Often those who experience PTSD try to avoid triggers, even people, who were part of that traumatic event.

- **Bipolar Mood Disorder.** There are two phases of a bipolar mood disorder: the lows (depression) and the highs (mania). The highs and lows can occur almost at the same time, leaving you confused with rapid mood swings. It's important that your mood history is reviewed to properly diagnose.

- **Postpartum Psychosis.** The most rare, postpartum psychosis occurs in approximately one to two out of every one thousand births—equating to .1 to .2 percent. It's usually very sudden, often within the first two weeks, but can appear anytime in the first year. It includes having delusions and strange beliefs, hallucinations, hyperactivity, paranoia, and difficulty communicating. It is often the most dangerous PMAD. Research tells us there is a 5 percent suicide rate for the mother and 4 percent infanticide rate associated with this illness.

I've included additional resources in the back of this book, including those related to PMADs, to help give you additional outlets of support should you find yourself or your loved ones experiencing a PMAD.

My advice to you is prepare yourself now and vow to be honest when friends and family ask you how you are feeling in the weeks leading up to and after childbirth. Remember, your feelings are valid. If you feel unhappy with your experience as a new mom, that doesn't mean you don't love your baby or won't learn to love your baby. During the pandemic, Postpartum Support International reported 36 percent of pregnant and postpartum women experienced significant levels of depression due to isolation. That equates to one in three women. I was one in three.

In the hospital, it's common while you are in the recovery and postpartum room be handed a lot of paperwork: release forms, birth certificate instructions, postpartum care instructions, simple guides on how to help care for baby, and a postpartum disorder test. When I was filling out my postpartum disorder test, my husband said something to me that I will never forget. Keep in mind that, although I'm sharing this, he meant no harm by it. To me, he is and will always be the most supportive person in my life, my best friend, and an incredible father. And what he told me was to not mark my answers too low, or else I might get flagged.

Please do not skew your answers based on fear. Answer honestly, talk to the postpartum nurses about your options and local resources, find support groups, speak openly about what you are feeling, and don't hide it from the world. Women have hidden their perinatal and postpartum mental health struggles for generations, and that's part of what has led us to the place we are now. A place where women feel scared, confused, alone and depressed as they embark on this new, life-changing chapter.

So, go out and find your own Lindsey, or just start the conversation with your family and friends. Reach out to other new moms. Be kind. Everyone's darkness is a different shade.

If you are your partner are experiencing symptoms common with PMADs, get help. Call the PSI HelpLine: 1-800-944-4773, or text "Help" to 800-944-4773. The PSI HelpLine does not handle emergencies, and hours are 8 a.m. to 11 p.m. ET, serving parents in English and Spanish. People in crisis should call their local emergency number of the Suicide & Crisis Lifeline at 988, or your country's local equivalent.

SECTION TWO

PUSHING THROUGH POSTPARTUM

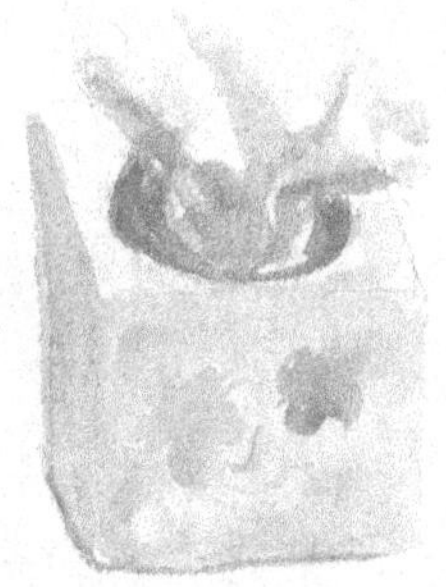

TRUTH #4

YOU'LL BE IN A "POSTPARTUM PERIOD" FOR THE REST OF YOUR LIFE

A baby is something you carry inside you for nine months, in your arms for three years, and in your heart until the day you die.
—Mary Mason

CONGRATULATIONS! You (or your partner) gave birth! It doesn't matter how it happened: whether it was vaginally or through a C-section, whether you used drugs or not, whether you were in a hospital, at a birthing center, or at home. You have now officially made it to the postpartum phase.

According to Merriam-Webster's Dictionary, postpartum is the period following childbirth. While the start of postpartum is standard—once baby is born—the end of postpartum is not so simple. Medically, the postpartum period ends six to eight weeks after delivery. (Unfortunately, this is also the far-too-short standard timeline for most maternity leave—if you are even lucky enough to have that.) Why six to eight weeks? Because by six to eight weeks, many of the physical effects of pregnancy have probably subsided, returning a lot of things about your body to their pre-pregnancy state. Key word: *physical*. Watch me roll my eyes.

Of course, you know better than this since you read the last chapter and are aware of the correlation between physical health and mental health. I only hope I can play my part as a small pebble in the pond to help create a ripple effect that will finally lead society to start talking more about the mental health side of postpartum.

"IN THE YEAR OF THE MOTHER"

This is my perception of postpartum: it starts when you give birth, and it ends when you die. Whether you are the mom of a three-week-old, a six-month-old, a fourteen-year-old or a thirty-year-old, you are living the "postpartum life." Yes, of course the exact meaning of postpartum changes based on the age of your child. Your emotions overall are hopefully easier to manage without the presence of raging birth hormones, but you are still in the period of your life known as "after giving birth." It makes me laugh because I think about the BC/AD dating system. In a biblical sense, BC stands for Before Christ and AD stands for Anno Domini, Latin for "in the year of the Lord." The system marks Jesus Christ's entrance into the world as a dividing point of history. For me, pregnancy worked the same way: sometimes, I feel like my life is split into BGB (Before Giving Birth) and then PP (Postpartum Period), also known as "in the year of the mother."

Jokes aside, the immediate postpartum period is intense —far more than people like to talk about. I've heard a lot about the three trimesters of pregnancy, but not as much time or effort is spent on this critical time, now referred to as "the fourth trimester." As soon as the baby is born, all of the attention, care, focus, and doctors' appointments are for the baby. Don't get me wrong, the baby deserves care, but let's not cast aside the mother, stuck dealing with the pain of vaginal tears, surgical incision after cesarean delivery, or hemorrhoids for up to three weeks.

And what care mothers do get is usually nowhere near enough. Mothers in the US healthcare system get *one* post-partum checkup that occurs six to eight weeks after delivery. On the agenda for this appointment: an internal exam, discussion about breastfeeding, and mention of mental health, and . . . what is your plan for birth control?

Excuse me, but having sexual intercourse was the *last* thing on my mind after a traumatic birth, PMAD, and dealing with my new role as a mom as the world spiraled. My birth control plan was abstinence. Let's talk about moms' real needs now, thanks.

The postpartum period can be a time of joy for many, but it is such a vulnerable time nonetheless. Women experience so many physiological, social, and emotional changes. Why don't we offer support, careful monitoring, and guidance to new moms with the same dedication as in the weeks leading up to childbirth?

Thankfully, progress was set into motion prior to 2020, and more has been made since. The American College of Obstetrics and Gynecology (ACOG) now recommends that medical professionals view postpartum care through the lens of maternal health. They suggest closer follow-up of women after birth and provide doctors with specific recommendations. They also emphasize that a change in reimbursement policies is needed to support individualized, continuous postpartum care.

While this is all well and good, it's nowhere near enough. The pandemic jolted all of us, but in my experience as a new mom, it really screwed us over. The "it takes a village" mentality and the ability to lean on friends and family for help and support—even just holding a newborn so you can take a nap—weren't a reality for me. Getting out of the house or socializing with other new moms? No way.

POSTPARTUM POSSIBILITIES

I'm extremely thankful and lucky that my mother was part of my in-person village and was able to support me during that first week. While the ideal plan was for her to be with us in the delivery room, she instead quarantined for a month (visiting only me), rode with me to my appointments just to sit in the car, and stayed in our home taking care of our dog while we were essentially locked in the hospital for four days. This way she was able to help me navigate the first night home, when my milk came in, as I was learning to breastfeed, learning to care for this helpless little being, while dealing with baby blues and PMAD. I don't know what I would have done without her, but I know thousands of women navigate this period essentially on their own. I was fortunate. I had free, live-in maternal family support and unconditional love. And even with all of that, I still struggled.

And even as I reflect on and share about this tough time in my life, I feel guilty about it. I feel guilty because there are so many others who had to deal with much more challenging circumstances than I did. But that doesn't mean that my story is any less impactful. The darkness I felt was still deep. I don't want to feel guilty about it. The experience of pregnancy, postpartum, and parenting can be challenging no matter your economic status, your family situation, or mental stability.

Postpartum tends to have a negative connotation, but

essentially, it's the story of our journey into parenthood. That story evolves over time as your baby develops and grows—just like how you develop and grow into your new roles as mom or dad.

Postpartum support could have infinite possibilities, and it certainly isn't a one-size-fits-all situation. It can be someone coming to help with care for the baby or someone coming to help do house tasks, like meal prepping, laundry, and cleaning. It can be going for a walk or taking a nap. It can be someone to text in the middle of the night while you nurse or socializing with a parent group as a playdate during the day. It can be sticking to a routine or breaking normal protocol and going out on adventures. If your mental health becomes a concern, postpartum support becomes imperative. Talk to a family member or friend, call the national hotline, find a local provider, or seek out a support group and get help.

To me, my postpartum was a wake-up call. It was challenging, but I grew so much as a person while becoming a mother. That first year, you can feel very delicate—easy to break and unworthy. Treat yourself gently and speak up. You are not alone.

TRUTH #5

YOU'LL MISS THE "OLD YOU," AND THAT'S OKAY

You are always a mother, but you are not only a mother. Remember that.

—Unknown

ONE OF MY favorite family traditions is creating photo books. When I was young, I visited my grandparents who lived in California every summer. My mom would pack up us two kids and travel 3,000 miles to and from New Jersey for our annual ten-day visit. Every time, I'd pull out all my grandmother's photo books in their living room and spend hours flipping through them, laughing at how young all the grown-ups looked so long ago and reliving celebrations with all my cousins. I'd thumb through the hundreds of pictures that my mom would pay extra for to send across the country, so my grandparents had a glimpse of us growing up. I'm grateful for the technology of today that allows me to not only send pictures and videos of my daughter to loved ones still in California but to video call them and have them interact with her. Don't take those moments of connection for granted, even if they are halfway around the world!

When I got older, I started making my own scrapbooks and photo books. I have one book dedicated to each year, as well as dedicated books for vacations, memorial books, and of course, the celebration of the "first year" of our daughter. I always tell Kyle that I really hope the next generation of our family cherishes memories and photos as much as I do, otherwise they're going to be paying a small fortune in storage fees for all our family photo books!

Just a few days before I wrote this section, my eleven-month-old daughter and I were in the living room, and she went over to the bookcase and started pulling out my photo books. She chose "2016," "2020," and "Baby's First Year." We sat together on the couch and flipped through the books. I pointed to family members and friends and called them out by name, some of whom she has met and others that she's only video-chatted with. She calls out "mama" and "dada" when she sees pictures of us. I'll be honest, this was one of those cool "out of body" experiences and a form of bonding that I only fantasized about. To reference the Pixar movie, *Inside Out*, this moment very likely could have been a core memory for her.

As we were flipping through the pages, however, I realized something: I hadn't been prepared to see pictures of myself before becoming a mom. It was strange. My transition to motherhood was not like how I had imagined it. While Kyle and I both became parents, dealt with lack of sleep, and a bloody aftermath, I felt like I was rocked to my core. Mix in hormones and anxiety, it was as if my identity was stolen.

MY "OLD" SELF

In the few days after giving birth, I looked at Kyle and told him I missed my old life. I remember his reaction clearly. I'm sure he was trying not to judge me. As soon as I allowed those words to leave my lips and witnessed his initial reaction, however micro, I knew he'd just never understand. He likely didn't understand anything that was happening to me internally or externally. He was dealing with a new baby and a wife who was essentially working through an identity crisis. We were both trying to fulfill new roles as parents without a clue. I was in pain after delivery. My body had gained sixty pounds during pregnancy, and I was as tired "as a mother." Looking in the mirror was a lot like looking at a stranger.

The "old" me was more put together; she was driven and didn't give up easily. She put others before herself, both in her career and personal relationships. She was sensitive but made strides to work through her own struggles. She cared about fitness and staying active, loved kayaking and going for a hike in the woods. Very independent.

The woman I faced in the mirror after giving birth couldn't use the bathroom by herself. I was exhausted from lack of sleep, totally let myself go, and looked like hell twenty-four hours a day. I couldn't even stand up straight for five days due to all the time I spent lying in a hospital bed, so unfortunately leisure activities outdoors were not in the cards yet. Nobody in their right mind would choose the woman in the mirror compared to who she was before.

What I know now that I didn't in that fragile moment was that I was going through a metamorphosis. It's a real thing, the name is matrescence, the process of becoming a mother. "When a baby is born, so is a mother."

BECOMING A MOTHER

I watched a TED talk with Alexandra Sacks, MD, who is widely recognized as the leading clinical expert on matrescence: the developmental transition into motherhood—similar to adolescence. She speaks to unrealistic expectations about the transition into motherhood: that it makes you feel whole and happy, that your instincts will tell you what to do, and that you'll want to always put the baby first. These types of thoughts are unhealthy and make new parents feel like something is wrong.

In some cultures, they say, "A woman has given birth," but here in the US we say, "A child is born." All emphasis goes to the child at that moment. Only in the last several decades has "motherhood" even been a topic of scientific research.

And this feeling of giving up yourself is felt across species.

Did you know that when flamingos—both mom *and* dad —have children, as they feed their young chicks, they lose their pink color? They are *literally* drained of their beautiful, vibrant color due to having to care for and feed their young. (This is a real occurrence; even my editor fact-checked this one!)

During postpartum, you might feel drained of your own "color"! Life might feel like mere survival. Making it from breakfast to bedtime. Hour by hour, day by day.

But guess what? Your color will return, just like it does for the flamingoes.

Even now, when Kyle and I look at pictures of ourselves from before our journey toward parenthood, usually our first instinct is to laugh and comment on how young, energized, and well-rested we look.

Now, when I think about it, I still miss the old me, from

before I became a mom, but in the same way you might miss your college days or miss being young and not having to carry the weight of the world on your shoulders. It's not so much longing for that time back again but rather grateful it happened and honoring that phase in your life. Maybe I'll feel similar when I become a grandmother one day—another life transition into a new woman and new role for my family! I'll start coining that term now: grandmatrescence!

I believe becoming a mom made me a better person. Ironically, it made me prioritize myself more, and not in a selfish way. I need to be the best version of me to be the best mom for my daughter. She deserves that. She deserves to have the best version of me to help her grow up, to help her learn, and to have fun with as we explore the world together.

TRUTH #6

YOU MIGHT HAVE SOME REALLY DARK DAYS

Perhaps the butterfly is proof that you can go through a great deal of darkness and still become something.
—Beau Taplin

To this day, I believe that I cried more tears in the months of being pregnant and the first year of postpartum than I have in the entire rest of my life. That just goes to show the magnitude of the emotional release I felt. You see, I'm not a big "crier," especially in front of other people. I experience emotions, certainly, but I just don't typically have a history of dealing with those emotions directly. I tend to bottle up my feelings and avoid confrontation—hence my mental break in 2019. But that last two weeks of pregnancy and the first month of postpartum, I cried *every single day.* I am not being overdramatic. I was overcome with sadness, sometimes feeling hopeless.

While I was still pregnant, I cried every morning when the baby didn't arrive. I had a fantasy in my head that my water was going to break in the middle of the night, so every time I woke up and it was morning, I was overcome with emotion that it didn't happen. Keep in mind that, by the time it did happen, I was ten days past my due date and *very* much ready to *not* be pregnant anymore. I've since talked with other new moms, and they said they felt similar. You are not in control, and time continues to tick by.

Then the baby is here, and the clock seems to restart as you begin recovery, physically and mentally. Then the real "labor" begins.

HOW MY POSTPARTUM DEPRESSION FELT

Depression. Before becoming a mom, I came close to dancing with depression but never fully experienced it. I've been very open about my pre-mom anxiety struggles, but the truth that took me many months to freely admit is that I had postpartum depression with my daughter.

Let's go back to 2019, which sucked for me on so many levels. My dad went through cancer treatment; tornados ripped through my town and a large oak tree fell on my house with us all inside; my sweet dog got cancer, had surgery, and suffered an awful recovery; and my grandmother passed away after a five-year battle with Alzheimer's. I understand the idiom, "Sometimes, you just have to go with the waves," but I was drowning. As soon as I lifted my head above the surface to gasp for air, I got pulled back under. On top of this, I was still trying to identify and manage my anxiety and navigate through panic attacks.

And no, I'm not trying to saturate my story with all these sad misfortunes to make you feel bad for me. I'm trying to set the stage that while all this shit happened to me in 2019, and I worked through it all and drastically improved my mental health, I *still* fell into postpartum depression in 2020.

I had a strong foundation and a support system in place, but so many women do not have this. Depression is not a one-size-fits-all darkness, and it's not a cookie-cutter description. So many smart, strong, and seemingly happy people live with depression every day. For many, this darkness lives on the inside and only occasionally can be seen on the outside. It's tricky to see.

Postpartum Depression affects one in five women within the first year of postpartum. Symptoms can be anger and irritability, crying or sadness, loss of interest in things you once loved, and feeling guilt, shame, or hopelessness. During the pandemic the statistic increased to one in three. It's me. Hi, I am one in three.

During those first two weeks I had some really dark days. One evening during the first week home, after our daughter went back to sleep after her 11:00 p.m. feeding, I just sat at the kitchen table crying hysterically. Kyle heard me, came out, and asked what was wrong. I wasn't speaking and just continued to cry. He went and got my mom, who was still staying with us at the time. I don't remember all the details, but essentially, I remember telling my mom that I didn't know what was wrong with me and I thought our daughter deserved a better mother than me. She just held me and let me cry. Eventually I calmed down and got some sleep.

After only four days home from the hospital, I reached out to Lindsey (my therapist). I had enough red flags to realize I needed help. I talked with her twice in those first two weeks, but it was going to take more time to find the light.

Kyle was only going to stay home from work for two weeks, but I *begged* him for an extra week. When he would leave for work in the mornings, he'd say goodbye to me, and I'd just sob to him because I didn't want to be alone all day with the baby. I did this every morning for probably a month. Looking back, I really feel for him. He must have felt awful leaving me like that. I certainly didn't make it easy for him, and I knew he was doing what he had to in order to best support us.

Being alone with my daughter was one of the loneliest feelings. Postpartum, long days, no sleep or idea of what to do. I have never had serious thoughts of harming my baby, but I can understand how some women fall out of hope and fall down that dark path of desperation and self-harm. It's hard to explain. I'm sure most mothers would never even admit to feeling close to experiencing it. I'm lucky that, because of all my former therapy practice and mindfulness, I was able to identify the feeling and understand that it was an emotional instinct paired with an irrational reaction.

Let me try to explain. You feel like you are at a breaking point, hopeless. No one can help you. You are on your own. This tiny human needs something from you, but you don't know what it is. You play a guessing game and run through all the options: Is she hungry? Gassy? Does she have a fever? Did she pee? Did she poop? Is she hot or cold? Does she need to burp? Is she hungry? You run through all the possible scenarios, sometimes even twice for good measure. Still, no saving grace. It's extremely frustrating, and top that with just complete exhaustion. I remember crying to her, praying to God, and begging that she would fall back asleep because, "Mommy needed to rest too." No matter what I did, she wasn't finding comfort. Your job as a mother is to protect and care for this baby, and in this moment of frustration it feels like you can't even figure out one single way to soothe her. You feel like you are a failure.

There were multiple times that I had to physically remove myself from her. I safely placed her in her crib as she continued to wail, and I left the room. Just for two minutes. I remember the feeling of angst and frustration at first. Then, I'd take a few deep breaths to regain my composure. I often told myself that it just seemed so much worse than it was given all the emotions and lack of sleep. Then I'd inhale, exhale, and go back in to pick her up and try to soothe her all over again. Most of the time she simply wanted to be held. It wasn't her fault, but it wasn't my fault either, and that is a challenging emotional intelligence exercise to deal with at 3:00 a.m.!

My darkest thoughts were early on: I was too selfish to be a mom. My daughter would be better off without me as her mother. I imagined what life would look like for her if I wasn't around. Would Kyle remarry? What would he tell her about me? Would he say that I was a good person? Would she think I couldn't stand her and had to get myself away from her?

It wasn't until a year and a half later that I learned these thoughts are considered passive suicidal thoughts. Experts typically define passive suicidal ideation as contemplating dying or harboring a wish to die without actively working toward that outcome. It's different from being suicidal, but if left unchecked could lead to tragedy. Suicide is the leading cause of maternal death in the first year after childbirth, accounting for 20 percent of postpartum deaths.

While I didn't have a desire to act on any of these thoughts, the daydreaming was frightfully entertaining, and during those first several weeks, especially when all alone with a newborn, the thoughts were awfully loud.

So, what to do if you find yourself engulfed in a darkness of your own? Speak out and get help. Asking for help does not make you a failure.

So, let's talk about how you can get help—and help yourself—when you need it.

FINDING HELP AND HELPING YOURSELF

Find the courage to take the first step. Many new parents are afraid to tell others they are struggling. You might feel ashamed or worried you'll just be ignored. You are concerned with their response: Will they think you don't love your baby? Just tell you to be happy or "snap out of it"? Think you are complaining or weak? Maybe they just simply won't understand, think you are making it up, or don't know how to help you. For many mothers, the fear is that someone will take their baby away from them.

Who in your life will be that person you'll be honest with? Establish it now when you are still expecting! Is it your partner, sister, best friend? Have someone in your life take on the role of checking in on your mental health and creating a safe, judgement-free space for you to share your thoughts.

You can also bring up the mental health topic to your healthcare providers. Here are a few opportunities and scripts for doing so:

- **Six Week Checkup**: "Can we talk about how this postpartum time has been for me? I have been reading a lot about postpartum anxiety, and I have been experiencing . . ." List your symptoms and be specific about them.
- **Pediatrician Well Check**: "I know we are focusing on the baby today, but I have been feeling really overwhelmed these past few weeks and really want

to talk to someone about it. Can you help connect me with someone?"

- **Primary Care Visit:** "I have experienced depression in the past and have been having those same feelings all of a sudden. Can we make a plan before I leave today?"

Seek out free resources. If you'd rather talk to someone you don't know, that is fine too! There are plenty of free resources available for new parents. You just need to know where to look. A few are even just a call or text away:

- The **PSI HelpLine**: Call 1-800-944-4773 or text "Help" to 800-944-4773. The PSI HelpLine does not handle emergencies and hours are 8:00 a.m. to 11:00 p.m. ET, serving parents in English and Spanish.
- People in crisis should call their local emergency number of the **Suicide & Crisis Lifeline at 988**. The 988 Lifeline provides 24/7 free and confidential support for people in distress, as well as prevention and crisis resources for you and your loved ones.
- The **National Maternal Mental Health Hotline** provides 24/7 free and confidential support before, during, and after pregnancy and is available in English and Spanish. You can call or text 1-833 TLC-MAMA (1-833-852-6262).

Getting one-on-one support is great, but don't dismiss the value that comes with a group. Support groups can be found locally in your community or hospital network, or nationally through organizations like PSI. Support groups encourage a sense of belonging. You feel motivated when you connect with others, especially when those in the group have shared experiences as new moms, a NICU parent, or a PMAD survivor. Why does this group setting work? Everyone within the space is equal. It allows you to become much more comfortable in opening up and sharing your feelings and thoughts.

Support groups can be in person or virtual. Did you know PSI has more than thirty different specialty groups, which are all accessible online? Their groups are conducted by peer-to-peer support model, meaning they've been where you are. Their specialty groups are based on specific PMADs, infant loss, fertility challenges, race, or family dynamic. They also have several groups for Spanish-speaking parents. Visit postpartum.net to learn more about their online support groups and how to join one.

Discover daily glimmers of sunshine—literally and figuratively. Getting out in the sun was a very helpful remedy for me. Sunlight and fresh air. It sounds cliche, but it helped, and it wasn't as simple to do in the beginning as it sounds. I started walking again the first time my mom watched our daughter so Kyle could take *me* for a walk. Then we started doing family walks, or I'd go for walks with my mom when she stopped by. We pushed the stroller or used a baby carrier. It was therapeutic. Eventually I got confident enough and even walked with the baby myself, with no support person. Wow, this was a monumental moment for me. It was so nerve-racking bringing her out in the world: remember this was the end of summer 2020, and COVID was still a very real thing. Find your sunshine, whether that is going outside or doing something you enjoy. Watch your favorite show, video call your best friend, practice yoga or meditation.

Leverage tools and tactics to help manage your thoughts. On October 15, 2020, seventy-nine days postpartum, I started using an app called Pixels, recommended by the one and only Lindsey. It's a color-coding calendar where you can rate your day on a five-scale model, allowing you to check in with your emotions and mood, and even add some notes to provide context. It showed me perspective in a very visual way. While the bad days seem really dark and overwhelming in the moment, those days are far less frequent than the days where I feel okay, happy, or even really good.

My color-coding system was:

- Dark green = Great Day
- Green = Good Day
- Yellow = Okay Day
- Pink = Bad Day
- Maroon = Awful Day

Here is what a good week looked like:

- **October 18**: Yellow. "Ok day went for a walk and got a few things done. Felt annoyed and upset that ego was making me out as the 'default parent' but got myself out of it. Very tired at the end of the day and anxious about her weigh in for tomorrow morning."
- **October 19**: Green. "Great morning, relieved from her weight gain, got to exercise and make food.

The afternoon and night were rough—she was extremely fussy, but Kyle and I tag teamed."

- **October 20**: Dark green. "Rough start, but got a lot done and kept my spirits up. Enjoyed some bonding time with her and went for a nice walk. I didn't get anxious when she didn't feed well, and we caught up in the end. Bedtime even went smoothly!"
- **October 21**: Dark green. "Had a good morning and bonded with her, mom came to help, and I got my hair done at the salon! I felt like a million bucks!"
- **October 22**: Green. "Accomplished small tasks but felt good. Only felt sad because of a show I watched that made me think some day we will all lose our loved ones. I stopped ego from a field day."
- **October 24**: Dark green. "Celebrated my godson turning one, weather turned out beautiful and I finished our home-made Halloween costumes just in time. We also tried a new feeding schedule that works out so both Kyle and I to get sleep."
- **October 23**: Green. "Good daughter and Mommy Day. Didn't nap long in the bassinet but cuddled up and even went outside with Leia. She was independent in her pillow and swing, so I did some small things."
- **October 25**: Pink. "Nice day with friends, tired and stressed about childcare, are we making the right decision for Kyle to change jobs? How are we going to afford childcare? Where is she going to even go?"

Here was a rougher week:

- **November 1**: Dark green. "Extra hour! Crazy poop morning, but quality time with Kyle in the morning. Got some things done and enjoyed the long day. Hiccup stressor in the evening (weight) but made a plan and not getting worked up about it at this moment."
- **November 2**: Maroon. "Had a decent day, but discovered she lost weight in the last two weeks. Stress and anxiety of it all is so frustrating. There's so much information out there and most conflicts with each other. How am I supposed to navigate it? Kyle isn't helping and doesn't know what to do … it's affecting 'us' too."
- **November 3**: Maroon. "Had a good day until 4 p.m. when she wouldn't nurse, and I got upset. I fed her my first bottle, and it completely crushed me. Ego was having a field day. I got overwhelmed and Kyle came home so I let loose: I wasn't tracking well for calories, I felt like a failure. How was I supposed to manage? How can I go back to work? Am making a mistake? Luckily Kyle helped me get my thoughts back on track."
- **November 4**: Pink. "I had the realization that I only have two weeks of maternity leave left. She is eating better but spitting up. The future is unclear and so much to handle coming up. Overwhelming. Not to mention civil unrest due to the election."
- **November 5**: Green. "Decent day overall, got some things done and overall excited about the weekend (her Baptism). Anxious about Kyle's job and his decision."
- **November 6**: Yellow. No notes.

- **November** 7: Yellow. "Long day but got a lot done. Kyle decided on his job, we cleaned a lot had a nice visit with family. Got bad news regarding a friend unable to attend the Baptism. Emotions were going well until that call. I tried not to let it kill my spirits in front of visiting family, but it was hard to mask being upset. I know it's selfish, but I just wanted one somewhat normal occurrence during this process to celebrate."

I wish I had this app ahead of giving birth to have a visual of what those first weeks and months looked like. This just goes to show that after the first three months, postpartum can still be very challenging to deal with. There is a wide range of experiencing good days versus bad days. It's different for everyone. I had much worse than these maroon day examples in November, but in the moment, on those days, I felt like I had hit my lowest point.

I'm happy to report that the maroon and pink days got less and less over the next few months for me. I continued to have some really tough days and still do. I know those days won't last, and I work hard to practice acceptance and let go. I also wish I'd kept up with the app because some days living with a toddler is giving me PTSD about my postpartum experience!

TRUTH #7
YOUR HEART WILL LEAP FOR JOY, IF NOT INITIALLY, THEN EVENTUALLY

Motherhood has changed me. It has changed my body, my hair, my breasts, my skin, my priorities, and my fears. But you should see my heart. Oh, how my heart has grown.
—Sandra Erath

I'M sure there are many mothers who never experience that strong bond with their baby. They went through the "natural" yet ridiculous experience of pregnancy and birth, and when they finally claimed their prize, no sparks of joy.

I don't remember if I felt joyous the moment my daughter was born. I don't want to sound cold, but there was a lot going on. I remember smiling when I heard it was a girl, and I remember feeling relieved when they placed her in my arms for what felt like five seconds. But there was no time to embrace the moment. That precious golden hour was stolen from me. There was no distinct period where we reflected on all of the pain and struggles that led us to this miraculous gift from God. None of that. We were tired, I was in pain, and we were essentially alone.

I love my daughter more than anything in this world. She is the best part of me, the greatest thing I've ever created—and I am quite the DIY crafter. But in the thick of it, in those first few days, you might have regrets in the moment about having a baby. You weren't ready, you are too selfish, you don't know how to take care of them, you don't even know how to take care of yourself. It's overwhelming, your emotions are spiraling. So, remember to take a breath. Your feelings are valid, this is a *huge* change in your life. You are not alone. You are not a bad mom. Take it one day at a time, sometimes hour by hour.

TAKE IT EASY ON YOURSELF

Now, everything centers around this child. When you can sleep, going to the bathroom, when you eat, when can you leave the house, how much time you have before the next feeding. If I had a quarter for every time I heard, "Sleep when the baby sleeps," I would be rich. Sure, in theory that sounds great, but what happens when your baby won't fall asleep in a bassinet and only in your arms? You don't dare risk the "transfer" to wake them up. There were so many days that I sat on the couch watching show after show with my daughter sleeping in my arms. Yes, looking back there were other options that I could've done, but in the moment that was the safest option that I knew she would sleep and rest, even though it did not allow me to sleep. It didn't allow me to get any food, and it basically held me captive on the couch.

Looking back, I wish I felt more confident to use items like infant carriers more. I also wish I had bit the bullet and put her down safely in her bassinet to get her used to napping there instead of in my arms. But I was a new mom, I was doing the best I could, and frankly, I didn't know any better.

I also felt so unaccomplished and lazy. Part of my coping strategy was buying a children's paper tablet "chore chart" to act as a small, manageable to-do list for myself every day. I had "chores" like eating lunch, pumping, going outside, and adding bullets to a daily journal about what we did that day. I felt so out of control of my own schedule and couldn't do the things I used to, so this was a way for me to take baby steps.

I remember sometimes thinking how challenging it was to hold her at times, but I didn't want to put her down. Granted, this was also an effect of my postpartum depression. I had one really, really bad day—September 22, 2020, fifty-six days postpartum. As luck would have it, I also had a scheduled session with Lindsey (my therapist) that after-noon. Timing was ideal. I even recorded myself and took pictures of that moment, because I knew that while I felt completely lost in the moment, it was just a moment. It would pass with time, and I wouldn't be alone in the house with a newborn. Kyle would be coming home soon, and then I'd find some relief.

It's in those moments that you might not feel joy or any emotion close to it. That's okay. You don't have to feel joy every minute spent with your baby. Heck, you don't need to feel joy every minute spent with anyone—even your dog. I loved my baby, even in those moments where I felt like I had nothing left to give. Maybe that's what true love is. If you don't feel any connection to your baby in the first two weeks, seek out help. You are capable of feeling love for this baby. You hopefully created this baby out of love and pictured the day you could hold this baby in your arms and express how much you love them. Don't let the postpartum haze make you think otherwise or literally cloud your judgement.

SECTION THREE

FACING NEW CHALLENGES

TRUTH #8
YOU CAN'T 100 PERCENT PREPARE FOR MOTHERHOOD

Making the decision to have a child is momentous. It is to decide forever to have your heart go walking around outside your body.
—Elizabeth Stone

MOTHERHOOD. You likely first started understanding what motherhood is by watching your own mother. Books, TV shows, and movies all depict motherhood in a wide range of ways. When the time comes that you're thinking about starting a family, while you're trying to start a family, or if you've unexpectedly discovered you are starting a family, you have your own notions, ideas, expectations, beliefs, and wishes of what motherhood will be like for you.

The majority of what I thought I knew about being a mom, I later found out was highly underestimated. I remember thinking, "Why am I having so much difficulty with this? I'm smart, capable, and successful. Why is motherhood such a challenge?"

THE BEST-LAID PLANS

You see, I am a planner. I like to have control and ensure I am prepared for what lies ahead, especially when it comes to my professional life. There is a joke that Public Relations (PR) professionals are great wedding planners. During my life at a PR agency, I saw many young professionals date, fall in love, and get married. I was one. They saved, filed, and shared event planning checklists, timelines, and roles and responsibilities built out before the invites were even sent. It's the nature for those PR brides and grooms to prepare for different scenarios, go over details with a fine-tooth comb, and be organized with vendors, guest lists, and bridal party names, contact numbers, and drink preferences.

Call me naïve, but I thought motherhood would be the same. Looking back, I've learned that the wedding day is to marriage as the birth is to motherhood. These monumental events that change your life forever, that is what we focus on, stress over, and create a countdown calendar for. We are very good at that. But what comes after the big day? That's when the real work of marriage and successfully spending your life with one person begins.

The funny thing is that when it comes to starting a family, you don't even have the comfort of knowing the date you will welcome this new bundle of joy. Heck, you don't even know when you will get pregnant. Sure, you can chart and take your temperature and look for signs of ovulation, but there is no guarantee, even if you do everything "according to plan," that it will work out as expected.

And even if you do get pregnant, one in four known pregnancies end in miscarriage. I'm sure that is not the kind of news you were hoping to hear. Eighty percent of pregnancy loss happens in the first trimester, before twelve weeks, which is why many expecting parents don't even share their good news until this famous milestone week. I couldn't imagine going through that great a loss so early on without my support system being "in the know."

If you are reading this and you are not twelve weeks into your pregnancy yet, please, don't let this worry you. Pregnancy loss is typically not something you can control. And if you have already endured that sadness, it was not your fault.

I've included additional resources in the back of the book that can be comforting if you have experienced pregnancy loss.

Through your pre-conception journey, society tricks you—once you become pregnant, all of the focus shifts to the due date. Thanks to the due date, you *feel* like you are back in control over the timeline. But when it comes to the days, months, and years of motherhood after that eventual day? Forget it. No number of checklists, scenario mapping, or research can provide you a foolproof plan for handling motherhood—or even knowing what motherhood will be. Same for fatherhood.

I'm certainly no expert on being a mom, but I can reflect and provide my take. I definitely was one who planned for childbirth. To save your sanity some essential planning is very helpful, regardless of what happens in the end. I read books, listened to birthing story podcasts, went to all of my prenatal checkups, took vitamins and tried to eat healthy, got recommendations from friends for baby registry items, took virtual hospital birthing classes, and researched all the growth and development stages throughout the pregnancy. When it came to preparing for the big day, I had my hospital bag packed, everything organized, multiple playlists created in Spotify, affirmations written out, an essential oil roller for stress, diapers, and clothes for the baby, going home outfits selected, you name it. Thanks to the advice of some moms in my tribe, I had a postpartum station prepped at home in my bathroom, frozen dinners ready to heat up, baby clothes washed, baby gear set up and waiting to be used, etc.

All of this preparation helped me feel in control. How could it not? I thought through everything. Even mentally—I knew the birth would be tough. I knew I would have weak moments and feelings of despair, but I kept telling myself that every single person on this planet is alive today because someone gave birth to them. I would get through it. The pain wouldn't last forever. I was strong, and I could handle it.

What I didn't plan for or expect was the reality of the pandemic and how it limited new mothers' support systems. I didn't plan to get induced and have my body unable to sustain the emotional and physical stress and anxiety on top of twenty-eight hours of labor. I didn't plan for postpartum depression. I didn't plan for the identity crisis, or what I now like to call my mommy-morphosis—a woman turning into a mother.

Nor could I really plan for any of that—not fully at least. Like I said before, the wedding day is to marriage as the birth is to motherhood. Motherhood isn't a moment in time, it's ongoing, and it changes and evolves in ways you just can't always prepare for—and that is okay.

Looking back on my own experience, this is what I'd tell new parents that you *can* prepare for:

- Practice asking for help
- Be honest with your partner and share your feelings
- Find the courage to still document the early moments (either photos or videos)
- Gather the strength to voice your needs and prioritize yourself
- Understand that the dark moments, while overpowering, are temporary
- Make peace with the fact that you won't do everything right
- Postpartum care, mental health, and finding joy

Reality hit hard. I thought I had it planned out and under control. I was wrong. I underestimated what being a parent really meant.

TRUTH #9

BREASTFEEDING ISN'T NATURAL, IT'S LEARNED

Don't cry over spilled milk. Unless it's breast milk, in which case cry a lot.
—Unknown

Disclaimer: I chose to be committed to breastfeeding my baby (even in times I should have given myself some grace,) but I believe every parent should feed their child based on what works best for them. This is my raw story and perspective, which might look different than yours, depending on if you exclusively breastfeed, supplement with formula, or exclusively use formula. "Fed is Best" always—for baby and Mom.

OH, the roller coaster that is breastfeeding. In my opinion, if your goal is to breastfeed, then you should 100 percent discuss it ahead of time with others in your life who have breastfed—whether you plan to do so for six weeks, six months, or two years. It is likely not an experience your partner will understand, or that your friends who don't have children will understand, or even family members who aren't on the same page as you about wanting to breastfeed. Sure, they can show empathy and support, but until you experience it yourself, you truly have no idea.

MY BREASTFEEDING JOURNEY

I worked at a public relations agency, and one of my clients for about three years was an infant formula company. While I was pregnant, I felt confident in myself that I was open to supplementing with formula. After all, I had read through research, participated in brainstorms, and heard stories from moms about their personal experiences and struggles, all as part of my work with my client. I understood that while breastfeeding is the gold standard, there are safe and healthy options to ensure baby gets what they need, and that mom is able to focus what is best for her. On paper it's clean and simple, black and white.

Enter hormones.

Let's first talk about my experience learning how to breastfeed, because I don't care what anyone tells you, it's not natural. You don't just instantly know what to do if you've never done it before, you learn it. And unfortunately for me, when you give birth during a pandemic, you don't have much support in the room with you. I'm sure the nurses and the hospital staff did what they could with the resources they had. But they limited time in the patients' rooms and focused on others who needed their care most. I didn't receive a visit from the lactation consultant at the hospital until my discharge day. That was two days after I gave birth.

I do remember the first time I nursed my daughter. She was immediately taken to the nursery after birth to be monitored. Once she was cleared, she was able to come back to us, and that's when I really got to hold her. That is what I was waiting for: that magical skin-to-skin bonding moment. They laid her on my chest, and she quickly found the nipple. She was a smart and apparently a very hungry little girl. I always thought I was going to be kind of weirded out by the sensation of breastfeeding. I don't remember feeling anything the first time. I think we were all swept up in finally being able to have her with us and grappling with what had happened the last few hours. At the time, I was also starving. I needed food, and it was close to 10:00 p.m., and we still hadn't told our family about her yet. They were in the dark and chomping at the bit to find out what was going on. Of course, she was in the middle of eating, but I felt like we couldn't wait any longer, so we started video chatting our family as I was literally breastfeeding.

I didn't know how to take care of myself, let alone care of her. I didn't know that she was using me as a pacifier, "nursing" for an hour at a time. I didn't understand the different positions and how to ensure she was latching properly. I didn't know what to expect to "have my milk come in," which occurred a few days later while at home and was so painful and emotional. Thankfully, my mom was with us, and she helped bring me warm compresses, figured out how to use my breast pump to get some relief, and helped Kyle and I keep our daughter from falling asleep on me and do her job to help get the milk out. She stripped her down to her diaper and tickled her feet!

In the grand scheme of my breastfeeding experience, I was quite lucky. I really only had challenges in the very beginning, and then, once she was two months old, we learned she wasn't gaining weight properly.

At the appointment, the pediatrician suggested that I

check my supply, and I did that by pumping before I fed her and then gave her that bottle so that I could measure how much I was producing and how much she was drinking. My supply was fine. She then suggested that we fed her more and made sure that she nursed for ten minutes on each side. The phrase, "You can bring a horse to water, but you can't make it drink," rings true here. Breastfeeding became exhausting and a very negative experience, for both my daughter and me. I would constantly try to make her latch, and she wasn't hungry. I was upset and emotional because I needed to reach the ten-minute mark. I'd switch her from one side to the next, back and forth multiple times until eventually we gave up or hit the twenty-minute mark. It was exhausting. Two weeks later, she still wasn't gaining weight like she should. Then all things pointed to me. My milk wasn't enough for her; the topic of formula came up.

We ended up discussing the fact that I likely wasn't getting enough calories to pass through the nutrients she needed from my breastmilk. And the truth was, I wasn't eating enough. I felt like I was barely living, holding a baby constantly because she didn't want to be put down. I struggled with trying to take care of her, focusing on my depression, and prepping meals for myself while alone in the house waiting for Kyle to get home. Remember that whatever the baby needs, the mom needs too—food, rest, cleanliness, comfort, repeat.

My new goal was to eat three thousand calories a day, which I tracked. In my mind, I wasn't ready to "give up."

Give up—why would I use those words? Pre-mom Colleen knew that formula was an acceptable choice for baby. She knew that the majority of new mothers faced breastfeeding challenges and the importance of finding balance and making sure Mom and baby's needs were met.

But in that moment, damned if I couldn't make it work, damned if I wasn't enough to feed my child.

At that point, there were so many natural or normal experiences when it comes to pregnancy and birth that were taken away from me because of the pandemic. I wasn't going to let that happen to breastfeeding, especially due to something I could control, like eating enough calories. In my mind, I knew that with everything going on in the world, with loss, sickness and worry, my baby getting the nutrients in my breast milk was her best chance to survive, should we get sick.

And the opinions of those who you surround yourself with matter in these types of moments of guilt, worry, and pressure. Most of my friends didn't have children yet, and those who did had challenges with breastfeeding themselves, way more complicated than what I was experiencing, and I felt embarrassed to ask them. Eventually I did confide in them, which I am so glad I did. I learned I wasn't alone with these intrusive thoughts. We made it through and found relief when she turned four months old.

I know I was lucky because I never had mastitis, supply issues, pumping trouble, cracked nipples, clogs, etc. My daughter never really had latching issues, she wasn't tongue-tied, and she didn't have frequent trouble settling down to nurse. Granted, she did refuse the bottle shortly after four months old, which was traumatic and disappointing for Kyle and me as we tried every baby bottle under the sun, with no luck, and eventually I just gave up and exclusively nursed. But overall, we only had about three months of breastfeeding stress.

So, why was I so focused on succeeding when it came to breastfeeding?

BREASTFEEDING BY THE NUMBERS

The 2020–2025 *Dietary Guidelines for Americans* (Dietary Guidelines) and the American Academy of Pediatrics (AAP) recommend that infants be exclusively breastfed for about the first six months, with continued breastfeeding alongside the introduction of complementary foods for at least one year (Dietary Guidelines) or at least two years (AAP), or longer if desired. Why? Because breastfeeding has many health benefits for infants, children, and mothers and is a key strategy for improving public health. Which is why many countries and cultures prioritize and support new mothers who choose to breastfeed.

Here is what baby gains from breast milk:

- **Personalized Nutrition.** As the baby grows, the mother's breast milk will change to meet the baby's nutritional needs. It provides a unique and specific formula of vitamins, minerals, and antioxidants. It can even change color! Many breastfeeding moms notice a color change when a baby isn't feeling well.
- **Healthier Futures.** Breastfed babies have a lower risk of asthma, obesity, type 1 diabetes, and sudden infant death syndrome (SIDS). Breastfed babies are also less likely to have ear infections and stomach bugs.
- **Immunity Boost.** Breast milk shares antibodies from the mother with her baby. These antibodies help babies develop a strong immune system and protect them from illnesses.

- **Anytime, Anywhere.** Mothers can feed their babies on the go. When traveling, breastfeeding can also provide a source of comfort for babies whose normal routine is disrupted. I breastfed my daughter during takeoff and landing of her first airplane flight, and it was the best hack in my "traveling with a baby" toolbox!

The benefits that baby gets from breastfeeding are often talked about, but not what Mom takes away from it.

Here is what Mom gains from breastfeeding:

- **Lowers risk of PPD.** In the months after delivery, breastfeeding lowers your risk for postpartum depression *if* breastfeeding is going well and you feel well-supported.
- **Quicker recovery from childbirth.** Breastfeeding produces the hormone oxytocin. Oxytocin helps your uterus contract after delivery. This helps it return to its normal size and reduces the amount of vaginal bleeding after delivery.
- **Increasing physical and emotional bonding.** Breastfeeding is a special and unique way to feel connected to your baby. Some researchers have found that the bonding from breastfeeding may help reduce social and behavioral problems in both children and adults.
- **Establishing trust.** Breastfeeding parents learn to read their infant's cues, and babies learn to trust caregivers. This helps shape your baby's early behavior.

- **Long-term health benefits.** Research shows breastfeeding beyond one year can help lower your risk of breast cancer, ovarian cancer, high blood pressure, and Type 2 diabetes.

It seems simple when outlined this way. After all, "breast is best," as many say.

Families tend to face many challenges when it comes to breastfeeding, including lack of social support. One of the biggest challenges is one that I am not sure I will ever understand: society (especially in the US) tends to deem breastfeeding a baby in public unacceptable and indecent. Oh, I'm sorry, do you want to have to eat *your* lunch with a blanket over your head or in a bathroom stall? Shaming mothers for doing something that you are literally telling them they need to do, and then calling them selfish if they don't do it (often because you shamed them!), is completely ridiculous.

All of the huge difficulties around breastfeeding are part of the reason that breastfeeding rates are lower than ideal and decline relatively quickly. Data shows that most infants start out breastfeeding—78.6 percent receive breast milk at one month old. The percentage dips month after month with many babies (55.8 percent) who still get some breast milk at six months old.

We also can't ignore the alarming breastfeeding disparities due to race and ethnicity. Non-Hispanic Black and American Indian/Alaska Native people are the least likely to initiate breastfeeding. Non-Hispanic Black, Hispanic/Latino, and multiracial adults are also less likely to breastfeed for longer than six months, compared to the US national rate. Why is this the case? Multiple interrelated factors likely contribute, including historical, cultural, social, economic, political, and psychosocial factors.

I also believe the dip in breastfed babies (aside from general lactation and latch issues) is because moms are forced to go back to work. The United States has reported one of the lowest breastfeeding initiation rates among industrialized nations, and it's the only developed country without laws that mandate paid parental leave. Not shocked by this statistic.

You try working a full-time job while pumping your breasts with a sucking machine and spending twenty-five to thirty minutes at a time producing milk, storing it properly, and cleaning the pump. Oh, and did you know that many mothers see a decrease in milk production when pumping? You know why? Because they aren't with their babies. Enter mom guilt and anxiety to produce, and "bye bye" milk. Do you know what they recommend you do to increase the flow of milk? They tell you to look at pictures and videos of your baby on your phone while you pump. It's like pumping porn. My biggest ally for being able to meet and exceed my breastfeeding goal was remote work, so thank you, global pandemic?

If you do the math, a year of breastfeeding equates to a conservative estimate of 1,800 hours of a mother's time. This isn't far off from a full-time job considering that a forty-hour work week with three weeks of vacation comes in at 1,960 hours of work time a year. Breastfeeding is only free when you don't value a mother's time or energy!

STICKING WITH IT

How long should a mother breastfeed her baby? "Should" is the key word here. No one should dictate what you do with your body. I remember visiting one of my closest friends after she welcomed her baby boy. She had challenges breastfeeding and chose to formula feed. When she told me, I had no judgment for her. I understood. I didn't expect to feel envious of her though. Envious that she was able to (from what I could see) put herself and her needs first.

I started reflecting back on my experience. Wondering how much less stressful it might have been to not be the sole nourishment provider to my baby. Sharing the load with my partner and sleeping in shifts to get more rest. Not having the hormones raging through my body. Being able to leave her with her grandparents for more than two hours and not worrying about getting back in time before her next feeding.

Breastfeeding takes its toll on you. "Sacrifice" has a negative connotation, but I would consider breastfeeding (including exclusively pumping) as a sacrifice. Sacrifice: noun; an act of giving up something valued for the sake of something else regarded as more important or worthy. I gave up my own needs and deemed my daughter more worthy. Many moms can say the same thing about formula feeding that my friend did. They deemed their own needs worthy, and that's something I have always struggled to do.

So, as my friend shared her story with me, I found myself a little envious. Part of me wished I was able to choose to supplement with formula and not be ridden with guilt. Deem myself worthy to have my needs met too.

Looking back, I am very happy with my decision to keep up with breastfeeding. As we approached my daughter's second birthday, I had a feeling my moments were fleeting when nursing her. I remember talking to her: "You are growing up. I love this time with you, but if you no longer want mommy's milk, that's okay. You decide." That last month, she started refusing here and there. The gaps in between feeding sessions got bigger, and then the morning after her second birthday, I nursed her for the last time. I swear it was her little gift to me. I think in my head, I wanted so badly to say I breastfed for two years! I felt like I crossed the finish line—oh, the little victories!

Find your own community to help support you in your breastfeeding journey, but don't feel obligated to push through if it's negatively affecting you or the baby. Your real support system will be by your side no matter what. Find a friend who has had similar challenges, seek the help of a lactation consultant, or even look to mommy support groups to meet other parents at similar stages in their postpartum journey. Remember, *you* are in control.

TRUTH #10
WORK EVERY DAY TO EMBRACE YOUR NEW BODY

*Every mark on me now, every shape that has changed since I had
kids, that's evidence of the fact that I am a superhero.*
—Kristen Bell

OY VEY. I'm not even sure where to begin with this one. Like
many, I struggle with body issues and body confidence. Yes,
celebrities and influencers certainly weigh into the comparison mindset. Social media certainly doesn't help, but I'm
happy to be witnessing a shift in social expectations to talk
about the taboo topics, show those real and raw moments,
and display what "real life" looks like for many, especially
parents.

At the time of writing this, one of the most infamous
celebrity families in the United States—Kylie Jenner—
welcomed a baby boy, and this young mother has an extreme
influence over girls. She posted an adorable and intimate
photo of her son's little feet pressed against her postpartum
stomach. Eloquently done, artistically beautiful in black and
white, capturing this tiny moment that so many mothers

around the world have experienced. The media attention that this one social post received is completely bizarre to me, an outpouring of praise her for normalizing the postpartum body. Don't get me wrong, I'm thrilled that she posted it, but why does it take a twenty-four-year-old billionaire to start a discussion about postpartum bodies?

Why do we hide our bodies and feel the pressure to "get back to pre-pregnancy status" after literally creating life for nine months and then sustaining life for up to a year (or more!) after baby is born? Culturally, this issue is a "tale as old as time" situation, with insecurities passed down from generation to generation.

POSTPARTUM BODIES

Becoming a parent can have this profound effect on you, what kind of person you are, who you want to be, and what value you plan to pass down to your little ones. I've thought a lot about how I want to be a role model for my daughter and what issues are most important for me to "get right" for her. Body confidence is definitely on my top ten list. And it's a tough one for me.

"Will I ever feel beautiful again?" I thought that to myself a *lot* during postpartum. While pregnant, I joked that because I was due mid-summer, I was going to be a giant, pregnant beached whale. You know because humor is such a *fun* coping mechanism when you are insecure.

Honestly, that joke didn't fall far from the truth of how I felt. After being forced into quarantine at twenty-one weeks, I spent nearly half of my pregnancy in sweats, working at home with no in-person human contact to the outside world, and too much time on my hands. So much so I made twenty-eight loaves of chocolate chip banana bread during those twenty weeks before baby came. I am not even exaggerating. Making banana bread or bread in general had its moment in the sun in 2020, but in my house, it was a rinse and repeat situation. You are probably thinking, well, you probably gave some of those loaves away. I gave two away. Thanks to basic math, this means we (mostly me) consumed twenty-six loaves in twenty weeks.

Now match the insane level of access to banana bread with my habit of emotionally eating a pint of ice cream for breakfast, and the result: I gained a total of sixty pounds by the time I walked into that hospital. I'm not proud of it. I also know it's normal to gain more weight than you have ever before while pregnant. I was actually doing quite well with my weight until the last two months of pregnancy. Then all hell broke loose. My body took a drastic turn—call it nerves, exhaustion from the pandemic, or just that unlucky third trimester.

My point in sharing my own body journey through pregnancy is to reaffirm you aren't alone in some negative thoughts you might have about yourself. There is nothing wrong with you, and your body is beautiful at every stage. Embrace this chapter.

PREGNANCY WEIGHT BY THE NUMBERS

There is no one-size-fits-all approach to pregnancy weight gain. According to Mayo Clinic, the "healthy amount" of weight gain during pregnancy varies based on, like, a thousand parameters. What was your pre-pregnancy weight? How many babies are you carrying? What health conditions do you or the baby have? Always discuss topics like this with your provider to understand your unique situation.

They say an average "healthy body" puts on one to four

pounds in the first trimester, with steady gains of one pound per week in the second and third trimesters. Therefore, a healthy weight gain can look like twenty-five to thirty-five pounds. Now I don't remember my stats, but sixty pounds was more than what my providers likely wanted to see me pack on! And why is that? Why is packing on the pounds during pregnancy a topic of conversation and concern?

A steady weight gain is what they want to see, especially in the second and third trimesters. But excessive weight gain can increase your risk of gestational diabetes and developing complications that come with it. The risks for Mom can include:

- Increased likelihood of delivering via C-section due to baby's size.
- Hypoglycemia, aka low blood sugar.
- Preeclampsia, aka high blood pressure during pregnancy (this is what I ended up with!).
- Developing Type 2 diabetes later in life.

The risks for baby include breathing problems, obesity, and diabetes, and premature births were found to be more common.

So, how do you stay the course and steadily gain healthy weight during pregnancy?

1. **Maintain an exercise routine.** Regular physical activity can do wonders. It can help you maintain your body fat, reduce insulin resistance, and help your body better handle the demands of delivery and recovery!
2. **Be mindful of how much you are eating.** The saying "eating for two" does not insinuate you

need to double up on your servings! Your caloric intake should only slightly increase in your second trimester—they say only about 300 calories more per day.

But here is my question when it comes to the weight conversation on postpartum bodies: I birthed an eight-pound baby, so where the heck were the other fifty-two pounds? The Mayo Clinic shares the following breakdown of an average weight gain for a healthy body:

- Baby: 7 to 8 pounds
- Larger breasts: 1 to 3 pounds
- Larger uterus: 2 pounds
- Placenta: 1.5 pounds
- Amniotic fluid: 2 pounds
- Increased blood volume: 3 to 4 pounds
- Increased fluid volume: 2 to 3 pounds
- Fat stores: 6 to 8 pounds
- **Total: 24.5 to 31.5 pounds**

I believe it. In a matter of a week after coming home from the hospital, I lost thirty pounds right off the bat. Half of the weight I gained was gone, with my skin sagging and stretch marks galore. My guess is my dramatic weight loss came down to the typical baby, as well as blood and fluid volume (I bled a lot with multiple blood clots that had to be removed), and not taking care of myself well that first week nutritionally. But according to the breakdown, I likely had an additional twenty pounds of fat stored that I didn't need toward the end of this pregnancy. (I wonder how much twenty-six loaves of banana bread weighs?)

YOUR BODY IS MIRACULOUS

I was recently talking to one of my friends, and my advice to her was to take the time to admire yourself naked in the mirror before, during, and after pregnancy. Your body changes a lot. Now that I've stared at myself in this post-partum body phase for so long, I don't really remember my bare pregnant belly or how my breasts looked without milk filling them up. All I see now are stretch marks on way more body parts than I anticipated, extra skin, wider hips, etc. One of my friends was once told by her doctor to just go ahead and throw away her jeans from pre-pregnancy because her hips expanded to account for carrying the baby, and they'd never go back to the width she was before. Wild!

Here is the hard truth that no one wants to hear, especially physical fitness and diet marketers: you will *never* get back the body you had pre-pregnancy. This isn't a bad thing. Your body just changed. Maternal bodies do incredible things and kick into autopilot to care for, grow, and deliver babies. Have you seen the pictures of what the organs inside the body look like when making room for the uterus and growing baby? The Museum of Science and Industry in Chicago has a cool visual depiction of what happens internally during pregnancy, which is available on their website (included in the resources section).

Let me try to paint the picture for you:

Your organs shift and squish together as the uterus grows, which is why heartburn and indigestion are often common pregnancy symptoms. Your bladder is one of the first to get squished into a smaller size during the first trimester, making you feel the need to use the bathroom every hour at an early stage. By midway through, your uterus pushes on your digestive system to contort it toward your stomach, making it push up at a forty-five-degree angle into your chest. By the third trimester, your liver and lungs are squeezed by your stomach and intestines, making you feel "out of breath." Once the baby is delivered, you'll likely see improvements to your breathing and general comfort right away. Your womb starts shrinking and by six weeks is back to its normal size This allows all the other organs to fall back into their normal spot within your body. A complete return to "normal" takes about two months. Fascinating!

How is all of this internal movement even possible within nine months? The pregnancy hormone relaxin helps your pelvic joints and ligaments to do just what it is named for—relax—allowing it to adjust to accommodate your growing baby. I'm not a scientist and will never really understand the rational explanation for it all, but wow, the human body is amazing.

Speaking of what else you might like to do with your body . . .

SOME LIKE IT HOT (BUT NOT DURING POSTPARTUM)

Let's talk sex. Yes, I'm going there. Sorry in advance, Mom and Dad. It's still appalling to me that at your one-and-only postpartum appointment, birth control and sex is a topic of discussion. I mean, I guess I get it—this is their one moment to meet with you, and typically couples aren't looking to have Irish Twins (babies born within twelve months of each other).

I still remember legit laughing out loud when my midwife asked me my plans for birth control. Uh, yeah, I'm not letting anything near my lady bits anytime soon, nor should that even be a concerning topic of this conversation. I'd love to meet those women, six weeks postpartum, engorged boobs, no sleep, raging hormones, who are eagerly waiting for the "all clear" to have sex again. Good for them, but that was not me.

"But Colleen," you might be protesting, "sex is an integral part of intimacy." Yes, and so are the feelings of safety and mental willingness to act. What if your partner's love language is physical touch? Now I'm a big advocate for love languages, but there is much more to physical touch than sex, so I won't accept that as an excuse. Thank you, next.

Scientifically, after giving birth, women's libido is at an all-time low. Why? Physical consequences, such as trauma during birth, emotional experiences, such as postpartum depression, and of course, our good friends, hormones. Specifically hormonal changes including a drop in estrogen or rise in prolactin. Essentially having a low sex drive for a period of time postpartum is a normal evolutionary adaptive response designed to ensure that you survive to continue to reproduce. Oh, fun! Prolactin also causes your breasts to grow during pregnancy and prepares them for the milk production starting after birth. This hormone helps you relax while you are nursing, but it also depresses your libido. This is biology once again making sure you remain focused on the biological investment you just made in your baby. Wow.

You might be one of the 95 percent of first-time moms who tear during vaginal births or 12 percent who receive an episiotomy during vaginal births (lucky for me, I can be included in *both* statistics.) This is a highly sensitive area of your body, and you *need* to heal. TMI—I felt botched down there. I discovered I had a rare skin tag due to my stitches and healing process. In short, my skin didn't heal the way it was supposed to. I didn't find relief until January 2021, which was five months postpartum, and that was only after two medical visits, a liquid nitrogen burn, prescribed estrogen crème application, and four sessions of pelvic floor therapy. And before I found that relief, sex was very, very painful. I didn't enjoy it; I was very anxious about it, and at one point I thought to myself that I would never have another positive sex experience again. (Don't worry, I was wrong!)

And on top of all the physical reasons things are rough down there, let's get into headspace—where you're at mentally. At six weeks postpartum, you are still in the thick of it. Granted the worst is hopefully behind you, but by no means is it an easy road ahead. Remember, you can experience perinatal mood disorders up to baby's first birthday, with some research even indicating through three years! At this point, you are likely meeting the bare minimum levels of self-care. Shower, brush, get dressed, possibly shave—if that's your MO. Everyone is different. If you know someone who got dolled up for date night at six weeks postpartum, anticipating a night full of uninterrupted intimacy with their partner, they are the exception, not the rule. The truth is you aren't the same person you were six weeks ago, and neither is your partner. So, to expect time together to go back to how it was when it was just the two of you is completely unrealistic. Talk with each other and start to build back who you are as a couple in a timeline where you are both comfortable to get physical again.

MOVING YOUR BODY FORWARD

The body you have is a powerhouse. Don't let the superficial desires to look a certain way take away from the sheer wonder of what *you* accomplished—another life. When you are ready, start to cut back on the craving binges and try to eat "better for you" foods. Keep in mind that if you or your partner is breastfeeding it is *so* important to maintain eating enough calories, that baby needs the calories from what you eat to fill them up. You can do more harm than good by trying to reduce calories to lose the baby weight. On average, breastfeeding mothers should consume about 450 to 500 more calories per day than their typical intake.

The majority of advice I've seen for losing the post-partum weight is to wait until after six weeks, when you see your provider for your routine checkup and get cleared to begin exercising with a goal to lose only one pound a week. You know your body better than anyone. Don't push your-self to get back to the level of physical activity you were used to. That said, when you *are* ready to start being more active or eager to be a healthier version of you, remember it's a journey. And it's not necessarily a journey that always reaches a final destination. Sure, you'll have goals to accom-plish, but now that you are a parent, it's much deeper than what the scale says.

Give yourself some grace and wallow in the early post-partum period if you need to. Your body will be put through the ringer, and for me, the innate human pattern of mental wellness affecting physical wellness repeated itself.

SECTION FOUR
REVELATIONS AND ADVICE

TRUTH #11
I NEVER TRULY APPRECIATED MY MOTHER UNTIL I BECAME ONE

The truth is no matter how old we are, as long as our mothers are alive, we want our mother.

—Goldie Hawn

I NEVER NEEDED my mother more than *after* I became one.

Full disclosure: I wrote these chapter headings early during my postpartum experience to jot down as top-of-mind topics to reflect on later. The majority of the time, when I sit down to write, I get emotional. I spent a lot of time avoiding writing this chapter, because I had an inkling that I would get super emotional as I worked to sort through my feelings on this and capture it all in writing.

Let me also start by saying I know of many new parents who have lost their own mothers, who don't have healthy relationships with their mothers, or don't have a mother figure in their lives. I honor them as they are strong and had a different collection of individuals as their support system and #momtribe. Again, this is my story and my experience transitioning into motherhood.

THANK YOU, MOM

Let me give you some backstory about my mom. And I hope you can reflect similarly about a mother figure or role model in your life.

Before having children, my mom was a medical scientist and graduated university with a bachelor's in science degree in medical technology. She worked in two different hospitals straight out of college and then wanted to join the local Emergency Medical Services (EMS) squad, where she met my dad. She'll say the "boys club" created extra tests she was required to pass before joining because she was a woman; my dad will deny it. She ended up joining a different town's Rescue Squad and continued moving up. She'll proudly tell you that her name is listed on a patent as part of a team of scientists at Ortho Clinical Diagnostics Inc. who discovered a method and reagent for blood typing. I couldn't tell you what that means, but it's still pretty awesome that her work led to something recognized by the European Patent Office! She was the eldest of six, so the bar was set high to be successful and make an impact at a very young age.

This was her life until the mid-'80s when she welcomed my brother. To me, for my entire life, she was just a mom. Why am I sharing this? Because before you become a parent, you should honor and appreciate the person you were before. My mom dedicated much of her adult life to raising her two kids, often setting aside her own desires and drive.

She nestled into her "stay-at-home-mom" role when I came into the picture in May of 1990. I was the kid who was breastfed up until I was eighteen months old, who never had to be put into daycare and never had to wait around for Mom to get home from work (just Dad). She was always there. She took me to Gymboree classes and Moms & Tots, was a "room mom" volunteering as a parent to support the teacher with activities or holiday events throughout each grade level, involved in Parent Teacher Association programs, and chaperoned class trips and school dances (ugh).

She started part-time gigs once I was in grade school, but I never felt that her jobs superseded her role as my mom—at least I didn't notice any stress on her part for tackling both. I actually have fond memories of days when she'd drop me off at school because she worked close by, and we stopped at Burger King to get an order of cini-minis: a four-pack of miniature cinnamon rolls that came with a packet of icing to dip it in. Delicious. To add to her resume, she went through non-traditional schooling to become a science teacher and has an impressive list of volunteer roles: helping animal shelters, aiding hospice patients, and currently frequents her local hospital as a "cuddler," helping hold and cuddle babies in the NICU when their families are unable to be there.

I am so impressed and proud of the woman she is, and I don't give her enough credit for all that she did to be present in my life growing up and all the ways she spent her time to help others.

Now that I am a mom, I look at her and think, "How did you manage all of that?" Even when I doubt my own capabilities as a parent, I'm often in awe of how others make it through and make it look, dare I say, easy? I know her experience as a mom wasn't perfect, but it always seemed like she put us first. But who took care of her? Did she struggle in similar ways I did? Did she have intrusive thoughts or mental health concerns? It was a different world back then: don't complain, don't show your emotions, bottle it all up. I guess I'll never really know. I'm just grateful she is with me on the journey now and listens and validates my feelings and needs.

Again, her experience as a grandmother isn't perfect, but she continues to put her grown children first.

I don't believe I was a troublesome child back then, but I surely didn't fully appreciate having my mom so involved in my life. Especially now knowing the struggle of being a parent and having to juggle so much. Honestly, even now I don't always fully appreciate her. Even taking her for granted. When you read this, Mom, know how much I love you. Thank you for everything and demonstrating what a mother's love is.

STAY-AT-HOME-MOM STIGMA

Let's break down some numbers. In the late 1960s, 49 percent of women were stay-at-home mothers. That percentage steadily dropped through the decades. In the late 1990s, only 23 percent of moms stayed at home, and 4 percent of dads stayed home. That means it took just three decades for the number of moms staying at home to go from nearly one in two to one in four.

The numbers continued to change as a new conversation started about being stay-at-home parents and the roles men have in raising families. According to Pew Research Center analysis of US Census Bureau data, in 2016, only 18 percent of parents did not work outside the home, nearly one in five —approximately 11 million parents. Stay-at-home dads rose from 4 percent to 7 percent. Nearly doubling. Thanks to COVID, the number of stay-at-home parents is trending back up, and quickly. Data shows that the number of stay-at-home mothers almost doubled from 15 percent in 2022 to 25 percent in 2023. Dads now make up 18 percent of stay-at-home parents in the US, which means one in five stay-at-home parents are dads.

Why are there currently more parents not working for pay now than in the 1990s?

Moms:

- 79 percent take care of the home or family.
- 9 percent are ill or disabled.
- Smaller shares said they didn't work because they were students, unable to find work, or retired.

Dads:

- 23 percent care for the home or family.
- 34 percent were not working due to illness or disability.
- 13 percent were retired.
- 13 percent said they could not find work.
- 8 percent were going to school.

What this breakdown tells me is that the bulk of the caregiving load still relies on Mom. More than two million women left the labor force due to the global pandemic, with many citing lack of childcare as a reason. Sure, dads left work too, but their return back after the initial shock was quicker than moms.

If stay-at-home moms earned an annual salary for all the jobs they perform on a daily basis, how much would they earn? Salary.com surveyed more than nineteen thousand moms throughout 2020 and 2021 and estimated the value of a mother's work by tracking real-time market prices of all the jobs that moms perform. The result? The median annual salary for stay-at-home moms is $184,820. It's clear, Moms are burning the candle at both ends. Stay-at-home moms work an astonishing 106 hours per week on average, which means they are working around fifteen hours a day, seven days a week.

"But Colleen, a working parent still does a lot of the same things for their family. Doesn't that mean they are valued more?" The data showed working moms spent on average fifty-four hours per week managing things on the home front in addition to the hours they put in at their job outside the home. Assuming they had a forty hour work week, when you add it all up they are spending a total of 94 hours each week split between work and home. Not including a commute.

I am not trying to argue that being an at-home parent is harder than working outside the home when you have kids. I work outside of the home, and it comes with its own set of challenges. It isn't a competition, and even if it were, there are so many factors, privileges, and nuances you need to weigh in on to compare the two situations that it would be impossible. But most people just don't seem to get how challenging (and relentless) it is to be on duty all the time.

The point of sharing this is that often society takes moms for granted, and while on my journey to becoming a mom, I realized I didn't appreciate my own parents and acknowledge the time they devoted to raising me and my brother. Something I now takeaway as I raise my own daughter and learn to "juggle" multiple roles and limited time.

FIND YOUR SUPPORT SYSTEM

When we made the trip home from the hospital (one of the most unnerving car rides of my life), Kyle drove, and I was in the backseat with our daughter. We pulled into the driveway, and I was overcome with emotion. It felt like a lifetime had gone by since we were last at the house. In a way, it *was* a different lifetime. My mom was staying at our house to take care of our dog and waiting for us to come home. Kyle got out, opened the door to get our daughter, and my mom opened the door to get me. I remember collapsing into her arms and crying my eyes out. This was the moment I needed so badly and what I was waiting for. A hug from my mom.

Our shared experience of giving birth and having daughters brought us closer. I now have a better understanding of her unwavering love for me. Her strong will to protect me at all costs. Her fear if I don't text her that I got home safely as soon as I get home after driving back from her house, while she is pacing looking at the clock and calculating how long it should have taken me to drive. Our relationship grew stronger and gave us more commonalities, which blends the child versus friend relationship now that I'm an adult.

Of course, she was very excited about meeting her granddaughter, but she was more attentive to my needs. She was only supposed to stay with us a few days, but I asked Kyle if she could stay longer, and he said yes, whatever I needed. When she finally left after ten days, and I was alone, it was challenging for me. When Kyle went back to work, I cried every morning when he said goodbye to me. Every morning —for weeks. But this was my reality and what I needed to work through as part of my mommy-morphosis.

It was such a relief to have my mom with us for those first ten days. An extra set of hands, eyes, and ears, plus just overall companionship. When your partner returns to work and your only companion is a newborn and maybe a pet, human interaction with another adult is a luxury.

I was very fortunate to have my mother's support. Just because I had this revelation doesn't mean it's always rainbows and sunshine between us. She underwent a metamorphosis too; she became a Grammy. And *not enough* people talk about the identity shifts when parents become grandparents, because that's a balancing act unlike any other. Figuring out when to step in to help, whether or not to give advice. After all, the brand-new grandparents have done this before and, "You turned out just fine." Yet all of that needs to be balanced against respecting boundaries set by their grown children, etc. Like I stated previously, postpartum is for life— even as a grandparent!

For those who don't have close relatives or friends that can regularly check-in with you live and in person, I highly recommend researching local postpartum doulas.

Postpartum doulas provide families information and support on infant feeding, emotional and physical recovery from childbirth, infant soothing, and coping skills for new parents. They might also help with light housework, fix a meal, and help incorporate an older child into this new experience. It's a great option if you don't have much in-person support from family and friends locally.

You don't need to navigate the early postpartum period alone. Find support from near and far, through loved ones or strangers. Do whatever is best for you and your situation. For me, it was my mom.

TRUTH #12
RENEW YOUR VOWS (IF MARRIAGE IS YOUR CUP OF TEA)

Marriage is a choice you make every day. You don't do it because it's easy. You do it because you believe in it. You believe in the other person.
—Michelle Obama

"I PROMISE to be faithful to you in good times and in bad, in sickness and in health, to love you and to honor you all the days of my life." Those are the words my husband and I told each other in front of our friends and family five years before we became parents. We were young and in love and had no idea of the rocky waters of life ahead of us. We thankfully made it to shore, relying on our partnership, and the sheer importance of that partnership and commitment is the reason I believe that, as part of your preparation for baby, you should revise and update your wedding vows if marriage is your cup of tea. A declaration of love and support would also work!

"I promise to be faithful to you in the first trimester through the third, during contractions and sleepless nights, to love you and to honor you as the parent of my child, all the days of my life."

My relationship with my husband got literally messy, real fast. When you and your partner don't have quality sleep, are essentially locked down in a room with no windows, bodily fluids galore, and are presented with a helpless infant to care for in a matter of hours, this whole experience can bind you together—more so than an actual marriage or commitment ceremony. We were both thrown into the experience and were basically "in the trenches." I like to believe that it bonded us and coming out the other side made us better individuals, a stronger couple, and a solid parenting team.

ME AND MY HUSBAND

I'll admit, I was anxious about Kyle being my sole "support person" in the delivery room. Remember, my plan was always to have my mom there with me. It's not because he doesn't love me or support me; he does. He just doesn't have the same emotional range as I do (probably a good thing) and doesn't always know the best way to react or respond to situations where I am anxious or panicky. I was also concerned with him having a front-row seat since this is the same man who dry heaved when our dog puked on our bed, and I caught it in my hands. He also had to sit down once when I had a laceration on my finger and blood was dripping out as a friend was administering first aid. He'll claim it's because he had an empty stomach. Recollections may vary.

But as we met in the parking lot at the midwifery practice —preparing to make our way to the hospital—we were both uneasy, I was extremely anxious, and he admitted he got emotional on the drive over, but we had each other. And we needed each other. True intimacy is twenty-four hours postpartum, while hunched over in pain and dripping blood in the hospital shower, as your partner helps bathe you for the first time after giving birth. He supported me in the literal definition: a thing that bears the weight of something or keeps it upright. He kept me up when all I wanted to do was collapse.

When we were finally back home, I remember telling my mother-in-law that she should be so proud of her son—because he was the best support system and father in those precious first forty-eight hours. I don't recall changing a single diaper. While we were both exhausted, he made sure I ate and was comfortable during recovery. Seems basic, but when you are at your lowest point, mentally, physically, and emotionally exhausted, it's everything. There was never a time I thought I had to act a certain way or be something for him. I was just me, and it was a relief to just have a steady and comfortable presence in the room, with so much uncertainty and nurses, doctors, and hospital staff popping in and out quickly to limit any potential exposure to COVID.

Leading up to the birth, we did not agree on names. Since we didn't find out the gender, it meant we were mulling over all possible options. Of course, we aligned on boy names quicker, but when it came down to the girl names . . . oh jeez. Some couples know their child's name immediately. They decorate the room with the name and refer to the baby by name throughout the pregnancy. Our little girl was "Girl Imler" for a couple of hours after being born. I was surprised by the clash of our preferred name choices. I started thinking, how could we not like the same names? Why did I marry a man who doesn't have the same preferences as me? If we can't agree on names, how will we ever agree on parenting styles? The intrusive thoughts came barreling in. In hindsight, the name debacle seems trivial. I reflect on it now and laugh. I laugh because I know how in sync we are as parents and as partners now.

Being in sync doesn't mean we are perfectly matched. It just means we parent well together and are typically in agreement about how we want to raise our daughter. Some of that stems from how we were each raised—the good and the bad. Some of it stems from what we wished we had more of as a child, and certainly plenty of it comes from (some of) the countless sources of modern-day information on the internet on how to raise kids. We want to teach our daughter to be kind, independent, and adventurous, to find laughter and love in life, and most importantly to feel safe in our presence and trust us.

Our co-parenting love language seems to be TikTok videos. We love sharing videos with each other, either with parenting advice, tips and tricks, funny games to try, or foods to avoid in an attempt to help lower the chances of dreaded toddler tantrums.

Another reason why I think we make a good team: we try to communicate often with each other. That doesn't mean we always communicate effectively though! One of the benefits of turning inward and starting therapy before becoming a parent was that it meant I had a stronger foundation laid out for my relationships. I had been working on myself and got down to the bottom of my anxiousness and intrusive thoughts. This made me start to practice talking more open and honestly with Kyle, explaining how I am feeling and what led me to feel this way. Giving him an inside look into my mind—a scary place at times. In the past, I held a lot in and didn't share much of the darker side. I'd close myself off and come back to the surface when it was all shoved down as low as I could push it—not a great way to live life or be a partner.

Kyle, when you read this: thank you for loving me and supporting me no matter what, adult diapers and all. You are my best friend and first pick as my life adventure partner. I couldn't ask for a better co-parent to go on this wild journey with. I've loved you since two weeks into dating you, and I will love you forever.

WHY YOU MIGHT STRUGGLE WITH RELATIONSHIP PROBLEMS

There is an entire area of psychology looking at the change in relationships when a couple becomes parents. You just lose the time and energy needed to focus and care for "us." It is too common. *Psychology Today* shares 67 percent of couples report a drop in relationship satisfaction for up to three years after childbirth. Three years! During your transition into parenthood, the frequency and intensity of conflict tends to increase, as do feelings of unappreciation. Mental health takes effect here too. In fact, a parent's mental health is greatly impacted by their partner's mental health. For partners, the strongest predictor for paternal depression during the postpartum period is maternal depression. The risk of paternal depression increases to 50 percent if the mother is also experiencing maternal depression. Yikes.

You might also experience the drags of co-parenting as opposed to being a couple. It's easy to lose sight of the original relationship you had with your partner because new parents get bogged down in the day-to-day tasks of co-parenting and neglect who they are as a couple. This is why many professionals try to encourage new parents to make time for them like saying yes when grandparents offer to babysit so you can go out on a date. Just have alone time, even if that means talking or making plans for something in the future. Of course, when my husband and I did this early on, we basically just talked about our daughter, and I even caught myself scrolling through my phone to look at her photos and videos. It's a tough egg to crack, but with enough practice you can regain your relationship again. Seeking help from a therapist who specializes in couples' relationships could also be a great tool in your toolkit.

But listen up: this part of your journey requires *intentionality*; you have to prioritize *you* so that your relationship does not get put on the back burner and forgotten. Trust me, doing this will also help strengthen how you parent together.

I'd be remiss to leave out the topic of sex. Frequency of intimacy for parents tends to increase as their children get older. In other words, parents with babies are having sex less often (on average) than parents with older children. Makes sense, since little ones not only take up a lot of your time but also your energy! Even when you make it to the golden "six weeks postpartum," you or your partner may have had other complications (like I experienced) that make you not want to engage in sex yet. It could even be painful to do the act. If you feel physically healed from childbirth, it's important to consider the context of all the competing demands of the postpartum period with sexuality, such as:

- Feeling "touched out" from the constant physical demands of an infant. This is common for those breastfeeding or just the constant need to hold your child.
- Sleep deprivation. It's amazing how you can even function on so little sleep.
- Physical changes to one's body. So much is happening with your body throughout postpartum.

- Lack of (alone) time. Even going to the bathroom rarely allows you solace.
- Relational difficulties with partner. Raising kids is stressful, and having a newborn is the jumpstart to that wild ride.
- Personal emotional struggles. Guilt, anxiety, depression, stress, happy tears, it all comes in like a hurricane sometimes.

It is also important to note that research shows that about 25 percent of women who give birth have a history of sexual violence. That's one in four women. A history of sexual trauma is one of many risk factors for birth trauma that can make emotional recovery and connection to one's partner difficult following childbirth.

HOW TO RE-UP YOUR RELATIONSHIP

While it is without a doubt that you and your partners' relationship will be impacted in multiple ways when you become parents, there are many ways you can support your relationship so that it transforms and grows.

So, what do you do if you find yourself in couple trouble as new parents?

First, take a deep breath. You are not alone. If you are willing to put energy back into your relationship, you will get past this phase.

Explore couples' therapy. Do your own research and find someone trained and licensed in working with couples. A therapist can facilitate effective communication and conflict resolution and promote a deeper understanding of each other's experiences and needs. By strengthening the couple relationship, therapy supports a harmonious family environment, benefiting both parents and the child.

Focus on your communication styles. Ever hear the phrase, "It's not what you say, but how you say it"? Very true. Also try and maintain a "we" rather than a "you versus me" mindset. It's not a competition, and as long as each partner is trying to do their share, you will not recall who actually changed more diapers or who woke up the most during the night to tend to baby in the end. Don't forget to validate your partner. This is a new role for both of you and a major transition. If you and your partner are struggling, it can be helpful to simply acknowledge your partner verbally for their efforts. Read up on the magic ratio, which is five to one. This means that for every negative interaction during conflict, a stable and happy marriage has five (or more) positive interactions.

Focus on intention. I know some couples who have a weekly check-in meeting with each other. They get down to business on the tasks of co-parenting but also check in on the emotional health of their relationship. I'd like to try and implement this more in my own life. We have a calendar on our phones that we "share" and put playdates, visits with family, doctor appointments, etc. Anything necessary for us both to know that will affect our schedule or our responsibilities as parents. I'm sure once our daughter starts grade school, more complex schedules will unfold where we might need to sit down and discuss the week ahead. Nothing wrong with preparing yourself by taking initiative with good intention!

Never stop dating each other. It likely feels that there isn't time for dating during the early months of new parenthood, but meaningful connections can happen in small ways. Micro-dates involve being intentional with your time to prioritize your relationship with your partner, even if for just ten minutes. New parents can plan to connect during naptimes or after bedtimes—no babysitter needed—by engaging in a shared activity.

I'll be honest, Kyle and I stopped dating each other. I'll put blame on the global pandemic or my postpartum depression, but it's a regret I have. You don't have to feel guilty about focusing time and energy on you and your partner. I felt like I was hyper focused on my daughter, and I know now that the best thing for my daughter is to have her two parents be present and loving both with her and each other. Even if that means she has a babysitter a couple hours a month or we ensure she naps in *her* bed and not in our arms.

Remember that intimacy does not inherently mean sex. You can have intimacy without sex and sex without intimacy. Intimacy goes beyond a physical act. True intimacy involves a level of emotional connection and trust that brings people closer, allowing them to be open and vulnerable with another person.

It's also worth noting that your partner can be your lifesaver when it comes to picking up red flags for issues during the postpartum period. Especially in those first few weeks, it's a critical time for partners to be on the lookout for signs and symptoms of PMADs and help identify when you might need help—and take the steps to get you help. When you are drowning in waters constantly knocking you down, you can't throw yourself a life preserver, but your partner can. For partners, there is a great book, updated in 2022, *The Postpartum Partner* by Karen Kleiman. It's a hands-on guide that is easy to digest, helping partners understand the signs and symptoms of PMADs. It's straightforward, packed with supportive information and specific recommendations to help partners navigate the impact of postpartum depression (and other mental health conditions.)

TRUTH #13
IT'S NOT CLICHÉ TO TRUST YOUR INSTINCTS

Boundaries are more about saying "YES" to yourself than "NO" to someone else.
—Unknown

YOU MIGHT HAVE ALREADY EXPERIENCED it—mom gut, parental instincts, that inevitable "feeling" you just can't ignore. You will know your child better than anyone, though maybe not at first. Remember, you are still learning and getting to know each other.

Regardless of how well you know your child, though, you'll inevitably be on the receiving end of a *lot* of advice, solicited or not. Personally, I know I was annoyed when people would give me advice like, "You'll know the baby's different cries based on what they need." For me, her crying was just crying. Some were more intense than others, but I never understood which cries meant what. But that doesn't mean I didn't know my daughter or what she needed. I did find my sixth sense when something was wrong—when she was getting sick, when she was gassy or not feeling herself.

I was also given a lot of advice that I wish I didn't follow or get so hung up on. The truth is that every kid is different, so what works for some might not work for you. And because of the infinite number of methods on how to raise babies, we find ourselves drowning in the mountains of conflicting information and opinions. At the end of the day, we are all doing the best we can with the information we have. Trust your instincts. You are in control of your decisions.

ADVICE OVERLOAD

When I say that you are in control of your own decisions, that is true whether it comes to advice from the internet, friends, family members, or even professionals. It's odd because even now I catch myself giving unsolicited advice to new parents. I always try to set the tone and add a disclaimer: "This is what worked for me, but you do what's best for you." I do think there is benefit in hearing stories and swapping tips and tricks, but the expectation that one method of parenting or way to interact with baby is the gold standard is just not true, and hearing that is toxic for new parents trying to figure it all out.

Ironically, here I am writing chapter after chapter of information overload. But again, this is my story. It doesn't mean I expect you to do things the way I recommend. And I'm definitely not saying you should feel insecure or inadequate for doing things differently than me.

Being a parent today, when you have the entire world of knowledge at your fingertips, at all hours of the day, is both a blessing and a curse. Everyone has advice, everyone has opinions, and you don't know what will work for you. You might try something that everybody swears by, and it doesn't work, so you get frustrated because, "Why does everybody else have an easier time with it than me?"

Here's my one tip: take a good look at who or what is providing the advice before you make a decision on how much or little you want to follow it. I previously joked about how my husband and mine's parenting love language is sharing TikTok videos. Friendly reminder that *anyone* can make a social media video claiming to be an expert or presenting false findings. Take it with a grain of salt and follow accounts or sites that have good credibility. That will help eliminate some of the noise.

You will likely be on the receiving end of unwanted advice on how to be the best parent. It might come from strangers at the supermarket or fellow moms at drop-off, and unfortunately, sometimes from our loved ones. This is when you should lean into your instincts the most and set boundaries to protect yourself and ensure your baby's best interests are considered.

SET BOUNDARIES TO PROTECT YOUR BABY (AND YOURSELF)

Trying to figure out how to set boundaries can feel tricky, and the difficulty level only intensifies when setting boundaries with family or friends. The reality is you'll likely make parenting decisions that differ from how you grew up, and sometimes, the people around you will take that personally. While your intention is not to hurt anyone's feelings, generally not speaking up is hurting *your* feelings. If you are on the same page as your partner, then together you should set the standard as a united front for your new family.

I saw a video that really stuck with me where they described how entering a marriage isn't you joining their family or them joining yours. It's both of you creating your new family together. Your parents and siblings are now "extended family," which means they are not the highest priority. Your focus is on *your* brand-new family—you, your partner, and your baby. Of course, this gets trickier when it comes to how you celebrate holidays, where you live, and how you want to raise your children. Trust your instincts about those issues, and if friends and family members don't want to get on board and support you, then that's on them. Don't adapt your way of life to accommodate others who don't respect you as parents. Even if you have only been parents for one week, you have that right. Remember that healthy boundaries communicate to others how each person would like to be treated, with the end goal of cultivating a thriving relationship.

So, what boundaries might you look to set as a new parent? Here are a few examples:

Visiting. You may want visitors in the hospital the day after giving birth, or you may want to close out the world and spend those first few weeks at home—just the three of you, no visitors allowed. Both options are valid. When you are ready for visitors, be honest about best time of the day, how long they can stay, if they can hold the baby, etc. Remember that you and your partner are going through a lot of changes those first several weeks of postpartum.

Germs. Whether you gave birth during a pandemic or not, this is a huge area where practically everyone's boundaries tend to get criticized, especially by those closest to you. COVID aside, a newborn baby is still developing their immune system, and limiting contact to germs is the best course of action. If you want family members who will be helping as caregivers to get up to date on recommended shots or vaccines, then tell them that. If you instruct visitors to wash their hands before touching or holding baby, makes sense to me! If your friend isn't feeling well, tell them not to come for a visit, and find another date. If you tell your mom she must refrain from kissing the baby as there is a spike in RSV, she should respect your wishes. Remember, this is your baby, and these boundaries are here to help keep them healthy and happy.

Soothing. I always found this one challenging. I'm not sure how to describe it, but as a mom, when my daughter is upset, I am upset. I've always heard that children are a just a piece of your heart living outside of your body. And I 100 percent believe it. When you are in your postpartum period, you are allowed to soothe your baby at any point in time, no questions asked. Your personal bond with baby supersedes any family member's bond with your baby. So, if your mom is holding baby, and baby starts to fuss, and your instinct is telling you that baby needs to eat, or be held a certain way, or be soothed by you? No apologies. You take your child from your mom and say, "We'll try having you hold them again once I feed baby," or once baby relaxes and falls asleep, or frankly just "another time."

BEING A FIRST-TIME PARENT IS FOREVER

My new philosophy is that every parent is a first-time parent for life.

Hear me out. You can be a first-time parent to a newborn baby, that baby grows, you blink, and suddenly you are the first-time parent of a toddler, time goes on, and now you are a first-time parent to a school-aged child and maybe even a newborn again. Do you get the idea?

I'll continue. Those kids grow up, and you are the first-time parent of two teenagers. Those teenagers go to college —yup, you guessed it—now you are a first-time parent of college kids. Then eventually perhaps they'll find their soul-mates, settle down, and start their own families. Now you have the honor of being a first-time mother/father-in law *and* first-time parent *of* a parent. Sheesh. Messy web of firsts.

Yes, I know it's not the same thing as that actual first time you bring a baby into your life. But I remember being in brainstorms when I worked at a public relations agency, and we were discussing products for new moms and getting pigeon-holed in thinking only about first-time moms in the sense that they weren't previously a parent, and then bam, baby is here, and their lives changed. That was the focus of the learning curve. Someone spoke up and shared about her experience bringing her second baby into the world and how even though she did it once before, it's an entirely different ballgame when you have another child in the mix, and how not many consumer product companies cater to that niche of parents. Parents who welcome their second child have never had two before, so suddenly they're deploying 1:1 tactics. Add in more than two, and you are playing zone defense.

We can even expand this theory: my mom is currently the first-time parent of a thirty-nine-year-old and thirty-three-year-old. She's never had kids these ages before, and she plays with an entirely different deck of cards when it comes to parenting her adult children, especially while dual playing the role of Grammy.

So, what can you take away from this mental perspective as a first-time parent for life? You are still learning how to do this. Give yourself some grace for not knowing it all or doing it picture perfect compared to your friends and who you follow on social media. I tell my daughter all the time when we are dealing with a challenge or frustration: "Mommy has never done this before. I'm still learning."

TRUTH #14

THE "FIFTH TRIMESTER" IS REAL

Instead of perfection, we should aim for sustainable and fulfilling.
—Sheryl Sandberg

AUTHOR AND ADVOCATE Lauren Smith Brody started a movement called the Fifth Trimester. Her book is a resource for new moms going back to work after having a baby. Some parents go back to work immediately, some get a couple weeks, some get a few months, but unless you decide to call it quits, the time will come that you need to leave your child in the care of someone other than you to resume life as a professional. Becoming a working parent was a transition I was not prepared for, and I felt extremely uneasy about it.

First, I'll start with my own postpartum recovery. When I was preparing to go back to work, I still had postpartum depression. It wasn't at its highest levels, but it was still present in my life. I also was still physically enduring pain from complications after birth, which didn't end up getting resolved until six months postpartum.

Next comes our ever-present "friend"—guilt. Guilt can

creep in and affect so much of your mental reasoning. I felt incredible guilt that I had handed my baby to someone else so I could work. This person was a stranger, not a trusted friend or family member but literally someone I found and hired online.

Why did I feel so guilty? I thought it was because I am my baby's mother. I need to spend time with her and care for her to have the best relationship. But for me—and for a lot of people—being a stay-at-home mom long term wasn't really an option.

THE CHALLENGE OF FINDING CHILDCARE

Here's what I learned recently: parents spend more time with children *now* than they did fifty years ago. While moms in 1965 might have spent more time at home with children, they only spent fifty-four minutes on childcare activities. Moms in 2012 nearly doubled that, reporting 104 minutes per day. Fathers' time with children nearly quadrupled since 1965, when dads reported spending only sixteen minutes a day with children. In 2012, dads spent an average of fifty-nine minutes caring for children. And these 2012 stats are from more than a decade ago! A more recent study found millennial dads are actually *tripling* the time spent with their kids compared to their fathers. So, listen to me, if you feel guilty, just know you are not alone and you are doing a fantastic job juggling home life and work life.

There is also an entire invisible load when it comes to returning to work: finding childcare you can trust, managing separation anxiety, pumping (if breastfeeding), sadness about missing out, packing bags, meal planning and prep, drop off and pick up logistics, pressure to be 100 percent at work, pressure to parent 100 percent, the mom guilt, managing outfits and laundry, and feeling like you can't do either role well. It's a lot.

Here's the ultimate question when it comes to childcare: Who watches baby? For my family, the plan had always been part-time daycare plus my mom twice a week for at least the first year. With COVID booming still come New Year's Day 2021, I could not bring myself to drop my daughter off at a daycare, so we began searching for local babysitters and nannies to come to our home to care for her while I worked remotely in the basement. Sounds great in theory. This situation allowed me to physically remain in the home with my daughter, I knew how she was being cared for, and I was able to easily continue our breastfeeding journey.

What I highly underestimated was the problem of finding the right person and the challenges with hiring someone to come into your home. It was incredibly difficult to hire someone. Childcare options are scarce as it is, and me being naïve, I only started looking one to two months before I needed coverage. I was in a rush to hire someone, and with the stress of finding and maintaining childcare for me to work (which I carried the mental load of), I can confidently say my least favorite thing about having a child is childcare. Nanny #1 wasn't a fit, though looking back I learned a lot and it helped me define what I wanted and what my expectations were. As we entered Summer of 2021, I was able to meet two lovely former au pairs who stepped in to help throughout the season. Each was incredible. The only problem was that they were making the next step in their own careers and couldn't commit to helping long term. After that, I hired another nanny in September. Overall, a good fit, she was experienced and really made an effort with my daughter through her development stages. And while we had some personality disagreements, I trusted her with caring for my daughter. Then she gave me her notice, as she needed more hours and pay than we could offer. I was devastated because, by this time, it had been a little over a year since I had returned to work, and I felt I was just constantly looking and stressing about who was going to watch my baby.

No joke, I probably reached out to one hundred people on Care.com and interviewed thirty candidates. I posted on Facebook groups, and I exhausted my friends and family for any connections or contacts they may have to find someone who would be willing to watch my daughter in my home. That stress was unforgiving. The new plan on the horizon was that my daughter would start daycare come June of 2022. I had to just make it to June, and it was February. Mind you, I had already started exploring daycares and learned of the immensely difficult waitlist challenge for most daycares in my area. Finding a spot for a will-be-two-year-old was difficult, as many rooms were already filled in the age group prior, so not many spots opened up unless someone moved or lost their job. As for the nanny struggle, I ended up finally finding someone for the last few months, and then my daughter eventually started daycare in July. That was a whole other challenge, but I can completely empathize with parents who drop their three-, four-, five-, six-month-old off at daycare, because leaving my twenty-three-month-old was absolutely gut-wrenching.

Childcare sucks. It's a big issue, as the "It takes a village to raise a child" mentality only works when there is a village to help. With more new parents living at a distance from extended family and friends, it's not the same as when our parents were kids, and grandparents, aunts, and uncles lived down the road or down the hall.

WHY FINDING CHILDCARE IS SUCH A PROBLEM

Childcare is a business issue. Many influential leaders are raising questions and advocating for more from our elected officials. Moms First is an organization led and founded by Reshma Saujani, the founder of Girls Who Code.

They identified the problem that while our economy is recovering from the pandemic, women are still being left behind. Moms are facing declines in their careers and their mental health. So, what are they doing about it? They are focusing on three areas: Workplace, Culture, and Government. Since the fifth trimester is all about work, let's dive into that one more. Moms First is organizing employees and executives to transform workplaces to finally work for moms. Bringing together companies to elevate childcare is an essential business issue, **because moms can't work without childcare. Period.** Neither can dads, of course, but no one is questioning them.

If providing childcare benefits was the norm for US employers, it would increase the number of working Americans with access to new or expanded benefits and services. Moms First even developed a playbook for employers, with APCO Impact, that lays out the daily injustices working moms face and exactly what we need to return to and thrive at work.

Here are the five main challenges parents shared about the childcare ecosystem:

1. **Affordability.** The Department of Health and
   Human Services recommends 7 percent of
   household income for affordability measurement.
   For 80 percent of American families, childcare
   costs more than 7 percent. A study found on

average Americans spend nearly 30 percent of their income on childcare. Childcare just for my daughter was as much as my house mortgage, and it was part-time! I can't imagine what families with multiple children under the age of five are spending on five-days-a-week childcare.

2. **Accessibility.** The majority of families don't have adequate childcare options available to them where they live. In some instances—both in rural and urban neighborhoods—there are three times more children than there are childcare spots. Your options are literally limited.

3. **Convenience.** I'm not sure any form of childcare is convenient. But when looking for options, especially in situations where you need to drop off your child, location and convenience are key.

4. **Reliability.** Backup childcare wasn't even a thought in my mind. Daycares close, nannies quit, family members get sick—then what? Childcare falls back to you or your partner unless you have extended backup plans in place. And guess what? The majority of that responsibility as backup care falls to moms, not on dads.

5. **Quality.** Is my daughter cared for according to my standards? Not always. I have found myself sometimes turning the other cheek, and that doesn't make me a bad mother. It makes me a mom with not many options. Her safety is always my number one concern, but I do wish she had more attention and stimulation in her early years.

Employers have a once-in-a-generation opportunity to reimagine the future of work. It started moving quickly due to the pandemic, and while many are shifting back into their typical business standards, working parents should continue to raise their concerns, ask about these types of policies during interviews, and create synergy with employers to shape the new "normal" of what being a working parent looks like.

We work to live. Let's dive into financial stress and the reality that we need to work to live. The hard truth is that we can't live on my partner's salary alone—at least not at this time. So, while I bared the postpartum weight of guilt during recovery, I also carried the financial weight to help support and provide for our family. There was no option for me to stay home any longer with my baby to care and bond with her. I had to return to work, otherwise we would need to uproot our lives.

This is the main trigger for a lot of postpartum parents returning to work. It's not a choice. For some, they are able stay home after giving birth and make it work. But 61 percent of American families are dual income, meaning both parents work. Working parents are a critical part of the US labor supply: Two in five workers—about 40 percent of the total labor force—are parents with a child under age eighteen at home, and one in nine (about 11 percent) has a young child under age five at home.

While I appreciate the strides women have taken to earn respect in the workplace and perform just as well as the men, our needs are not the same—especially when it comes to bringing life into the world. Parental leave benefits need to be updated to reflect the modern, flexible society we have uncovered post pandemic—especially in the corporate world, where benefits typically are more forthcoming and in sync with trends of what employees want, to help retention and talent attraction.

Because there is no federal law for new parents and parental leave, it's left to the states. As of January 2024, California, Colorado, Connecticut, Delaware, Hawaii, Illinois, Maryland, New Jersey, New York, Puerto Rico, Rhode Island, Washington, and Washington, DC, have laws that mandate paid leave for an employee's own serious health condition or disability—like giving birth. That leaves thirty-nine states—the majority of the US population—that either goes unpaid, relies on employers' policies, or has "no other choice" but to return to work, some immediately following giving birth.

This is inhumane. It boggles my mind that the same states that don't mandate paid leave have some of the most outrageous laws. Did you know it's illegal to live on a boat for more than thirty days in the state of Georgia? In Kansas, tire screeching is banned. In Louisiana, it's considered harassment to send an unprompted pizza to someone. You could get arrested for sitting or lying down on public sidewalks in Reno, Nevada. In Vermont, it's technically mandatory for women to get written permission from their husbands if they want to opt for false teeth. These are all rules that were proposed, voted on, and written into state law! Yet our state governments can't protect and support professionals who want to have a family. Sheesh.

GETTING BACK TO WORK

After becoming a parent, I discovered that my values and priorities shifted drastically when it was time to emerge as a working professional again. I needed to figure out how to divide my time between my family and my job. Before I went out on maternity leave, I was very ambitious, proud of my work, and led a team. During postpartum, I lost my desire to do more than what was required of me, and I kept my head down. I was an individual contributor, with no direct reports, and didn't feel much of any ambition to further build my career.

I also jumped in the deep end with both feet when it came time for my transition into the fifth trimester. I had been trying to land a new job for a few years, and an opportunity presented itself literally as I scrolled my phone, a week into postpartum, while taking a sitz bath. If you know, you know. It led to me returning to work after maternity leave only to give my notice three days later. I wouldn't necessarily recommend changing jobs during the early postpartum period, but for me it was a better decision to help take care of my mental health. In my new position I was a fully remote employee, I had no direct reports to mentor, and I spoke candidly during my interview process about being a new mom and how flexibility was vital.

I navigated working with a new manager (one who I knew, at least, from my former job), a new company, *and* a new industry, all while dealing with the anxieties of PPD, the stress of childcare concerns, and learning how to be a mom. It was *a lot*. I certainly didn't get it perfect, and as I was trying to piece together my new normal, I ended up seeking the help of an incredible career coach, Becca Carnahan.

I stumbled on Becca's Facebook page late one night in October of 2021 while I was stressed out, sitting on my kitchen floor, and googling "career coach for new mom." I read through her "about me," watched her YouTube videos, and read through testimonials of women she helped—specifically millennial moms. She seemed so approachable, super knowledgeable, and I just instantly connected with her. I emailed her immediately, asking for a consultation and telling her the following:

I also want to share a bit more about me to help paint the picture of where I'm at:

- *I'm 31 years old, I've always been ambitious and career driven.*
- *I worked at a public relations agency for nearly 8 years.*
- *I became a "pandemic new mom" in 2020.*
- *Going back to work and being a new mom threw me for a loop.*
- *I ended up changing jobs last December.*
- *I don't feel ambitious in my current role and don't align with the senior leadership team.*
- *Feeling stuck and unmotivated, just recently got passed over for a big job opportunity.*
- *I'm not really sure what I want to do anymore, I'm having second thoughts about my career path.*

She responded, of course, with willingness to talk with me more, but added in her note:

... And I want to tell you that while everyone has their own unique background, so many of the women I work with share parts of your story in regard to becoming a new mom, rethinking their role, and wanting to make a change but not sure what that is. There is absolutely a way to get unstuck and career coaching can be a huge help—I know it was for me as a new mom 6 years ago. (Insert sigh of relief here!)

Oh, how I needed to hear that. I chatted with Becca and ended up registering for her group coaching program, where I reflected and learned so much about myself, my values, and my skillset. Six months later, I accepted a job offer. Ironically enough, it was similar circumstances to the job I started earlier in postpartum—working for a new manager who I knew from a former organization, a new company, and a new industry—but I was so much more confident, not only of what I wanted out of a career move but who I was: a working mom.

I am so grateful to Becca. Much like Lindsey, she acknowledged me, supported me, and became one of my greatest allies during my postpartum journey.

Just to recap: the first three trimesters are all about nurturing baby on the inside. The fourth trimester is nurturing yourself during your transition as a new parent, and for many, the fifth trimester is integrating back as a working member of society. I've thought about what a sixth trimester would look like, and all I can think of is just enjoying the new stage of your life before baby turns one and you get thrown into the trenches of toddlerhood! Ha!

SECTION FIVE

ONWARD AND UPWARD

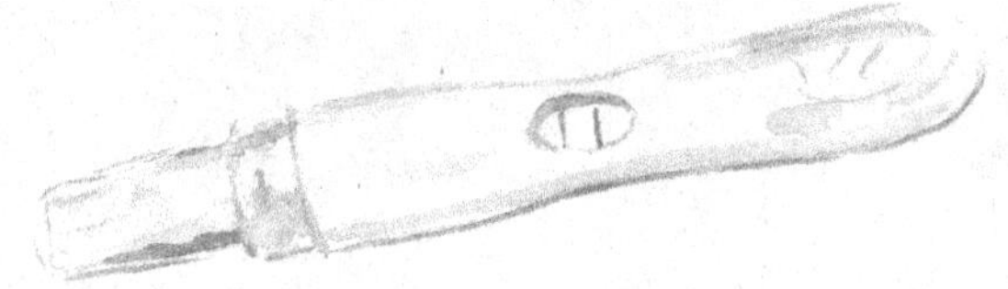

TRUTH #15
YOU HAVE AN IMPORTANT ROLE NOW

We struggle with insecurities because we compare our behind the scenes with everyone else's highlight reel.
—Steven Furtick

I FIRST SAW this chapter's quote on Instagram, and I thought, Dang, this sums it up. I remember seeing gorgeous photos of women in the hospital with their babies after giving birth. They looked fantastic. I would then pull up on my phone a few photos I have of myself, and I looked completely miserable. I need to constantly remind myself, Others are showing their highlight reel, meanwhile mine was the raw, unedited, behind-the-scenes footage that people typically keep under lock and key. The pattern doesn't stop either as you head toward baby's first year and beyond. We see photos of smiling babies, cooperating kids, clean houses, perfect partners . . . It goes on and on. After all, who wants to show off their mess, their tears, or their struggles with the world? Who wants to show something so real?

LET'S GET REAL

This lack of "realness" on social media is creating these unrealistic expectations of pregnancy, birth, and parenthood. Much like how love scenes in the movies do. We can't live up to the orchestrated and edited experience. Yet we constantly compare ourselves to it almost every day.

So, what can we do? We can start by simply sharing our own experiences—all of them. The good and the bad. It doesn't need to be a 50/50 balance, but don't fool yourself into thinking that showing only the good moments will make you feel better. I've found more support and validation from those I'm connected with on social media when I shared the hard moments. I leverage the "close friends" feature on Instagram to vent from time to time, ask for help or advice, or share those tougher moments with other parents who get it, so that I don't feel like I am the only one having a rough time at a certain stage of my daughter's life. It is incredible to have other moms and dads message me and share how they helped baby learn to self soothe or that they also got upset when they changed out the clothes in their baby's dresser with the next size up. These moments, while they maybe feel insignificant to share on social and likely might not get as high of engagement, can make the biggest impact. "I've been there. It's a phase and it sucks, but hang in there. You are doing great!"

Let's allow the current generation of parents to feel safe enough to share the real moments, real struggles, and real feelings, because everyone goes through it. One day or the next. No one is invincible to the trials and tribulations of being a new parent. And word to the wise, if you follow a celebrity, influencer, friend, or acquaintance on social, and their content makes you think less of yourself, unfollow them. Your mental health will thank you later.

I remember feeling so negative during my early postpartum days and asking friends who had kids already, "Why didn't you tell me about this? Why is it so wild?" And the answer, "Well, then people wouldn't have kids." Then you'd hear, "But it gets better; it's a phase." When you are in the thick of it, though, the phase is the longest moment of your life, with no end in sight. Having a community of people who are also in the thick of it, whether in your life or on social media, will have positive effects on how you roll with the punches. So, don't sugarcoat life as a new parent. Be real. Share the ups and downs, highs and lows.

And if you aren't active on social media, that's totally fine! You can still support new moms by talking about your experience with friends, colleagues, neighbors—really anyone you want. Find a support group or local mom community to share knowledge and vent as baby grows and develops through the various stages and ages. This kind of support is needed not only in the newborn postpartum stage but toddlerhood, adolescence, the teenage years . . . you get the gist.

THE LOVE LANGUAGES OF POSTPARTUM SUPPORT

What else can you do? New parents never forget who showed up for them—and I mean *really* showed up for them—when they were deep in the trenches of postpartum life. Ever heard of *The Five Love Languages* by Gary Chapman? Those same principles for relationships can be true for friendships: Words of Affirmation, Acts of Service, Quality Time, Receiving Gifts, and Physical Touch. Once you go through postpartum, you have unique insight and experience to be able to leverage to help others going through postpartum. Lean in, offer a hand, and have a conversation to help understand what support looks like to them.

Words of Affirmation: Here are some examples of what to say to new parents who appreciate verbal encouragement and validation:

- I'm so proud of you
- I see how much you're doing, and I really appreciate you.
- Your/our baby is so lucky to have you as a mom/dad/parent
- I'm in awe of your strength, but I'm here to help carry the load
- I'm on your team
- We can get through this together - let me support you with this
- What would the most helpful thing for you right now? I'll make it happen!

Acts of Service: Here are some ways you can support new parents through action:

- Bring or drop off groceries
- Help with older children
- Help with laundry, dishes, or cleaning the house
- Be their support person, listen to them, and let them know that their feelings and emotions are valid
- Bring them nourishing and warm meals
- Support them in any way so they can rest, bathe, relax, or take a break whenever they need to

- Offer to help with pets

Quality Time: Here are some example questions to ask a new parent to engage in conversations that enable them to feel seen and heard:

- How are you feeling emotionally?
- What chores or errands can I help you with?
- How are you sleeping and eating?
- How are you healing physically?
- What do you like or dislike about parenthood so far?
- Do you want to talk about your birthing experience?

Receiving Gifts: Typically, babies get flooded with gifts from friends and family when they arrive: flowers, cards, leftover items from the registry, diapers, clothes, etc. But what about gifts that help the parents through postpartum? Here are a few gift ideas:

- Gift card for food delivery service or a local restaurant that offers take out
- Amazon gift card
- Meal kit subscription
- Certificate for a cleaning service
- Postpartum doula (talk to the parent first before making arrangements)
- Postpartum essentials basket stocked with items like witch hazel pads, ibuprofen, sanitary napkins, Epsom salts, etc
- Spa gift card

Physical Touch: Take the popular advice on this one with a grain of salt, as supporting friends doesn't always look the same as supporting your partner when it comes to physical touch.

- Ask them if they'd like a hug
- Hold your friend's hand or place your hand on their shoulder
- Sit next to them on the couch while watching TV
- Go for a walk together

Maybe you are thinking, "I don't have anyone in my life currently in the postpartum phase of life. What can I do?"

Do your part to help break the cycle. It's okay if motherhood or fatherhood isn't exactly what you expected. It is okay to admit it's hard. It's okay to ask for help when you need a break. What's not okay is anyone judging you (or you judging them) for how this new transition of life makes you feel. We will all experience becoming a parent differently, and that's okay too.

Remember that being a parent can sometimes be heavy. We need to support one another and lift each other up. It's not a comparison game. We all have different circumstances and dynamics, but what we all have in common is that we are parents, and we are raising the next generation together. Remember to model kindness, and remember that everyone's journey is unique and different. No judgement zones.

TRUTH #16
THE UNITED STATES NEEDS TO LEVEL UP POSTPARTUM CARE

A movement only takes form from that first act. Exploring a curiosity, or a real passion, and being motivated by a desire to solve something—that's really the best way.
—Reshma Saujani

OVERALL, the United States spends the most money in the world on healthcare per person—though this isn't technically a good thing. The rising cost of healthcare makes it barely affordable to some and not at all to many. Despite the focus of dollars pouring into the healthcare system, in regard to women's health, we typically rank last when compared to other wealthy nations. In fact, US women have the highest rate of maternal mortality among high-income countries, which has been steadily rising in the past decades. Terrifying! Many advocates recommend looking toward the health systems of countries with low rates. For example, in many other countries, maternal care is free at the point of delivery, including postpartum care. Most countries also deliver maternal care in primary care or community-based settings by nurses or midwives, rather than in specialty or inpatient settings using obstetricians.

The US remains the only country in the developed world that does not guarantee paid maternity leave, despite International Labor Organization standards recommending that new mothers should be provided at least two-thirds of previous earnings for a minimum of fourteen weeks.

What can we learn from other countries, and how can we make a real impact to change things in the US?

POSTPARTUM CARE AROUND THE WORLD

When it comes to postpartum care, there is no need to necessarily reinvent the wheel. Luckily, there are ideas and models for postpartum care all over the world that we can take inspiration from. This isn't a one-size-fits-all situation to solving the postpartum crisis here in the US, but learning from others can give us a decent start. Here are some of the biggest things we can do to change our situation and truly support postpartum health.

Prepare for Postpartum Care

Americans like to focus on the pregnancy preparation—things like hosting baby showers and designing the nursery. But many postpartum-positive countries incorporate post-partum education into prenatal care.

In the Netherlands and Belgium, postpartum planning begins around thirty-four weeks. In Spain, you'll receive "mother's passport" and check in with a community midwife monthly. Finland's maternity package is unbeatable: once mothers are twenty-two weeks pregnant, they can apply for a free box through the Finnish social security system. The box is filled with sixty-three essentials for baby, and the box can double as a bed for baby.

And American-based research has shown the value and power prenatal care has. A 2013 study based in Greensboro, North Carolina, concluded doulas have a positive impact on healthy births and that including a doula in prenatal care reduced adverse birth outcomes while benefiting mothers, babies, and the medical community as a whole. I don't think I met one person who used a doula when I was pregnant. Why is that? I think we are often left to simply come up with our own birth plan, or be told what our birth plan will be, in the current healthcare system—not truly knowing our options or what is most beneficial for us.

Take a Moment to Pause after Birth

Did you know many cultures have special postnatal customs, including special diet, isolation, rest, and assistance for the mother? Let's take a look:

- Mexico has *cuarentena*, a thirty-day rest period with family.
- China has a similar practice of "doing the month."
- Japanese mothers-to-be move back home for *satogaeri bunben*—returning to stay at their own mother's house from thirty-two to thirty-five weeks of pregnancy until a few months' postpartum.
- Korean families practice a three-week course of seclusion (and seaweed soup) called *saam-chil-il*.
- Eastern European women are secluded for the first month after birth.

- Throughout Latin America, in addition to secluded rest, postpartum body massage and abdominal binding are common.

In the US, six weeks is our timeline to bounce back after having a baby, and it typically marks the end of our maternal support in the system. Now, not all these cultural quarantines and rituals are necessarily recommended in the modern day, especially regarding mental health and hygiene. Still, there's one very important takeaway for Americans here: try to slow down. Lower your expectations on what you can and should accomplish in the first several months after giving birth.

Redefine Recovery

Often, we are the sole educator and provider of our own postpartum care, and that is extremely challenging and even dangerous, as we don't know what is common or normal in recovery. Developed countries with the lowest maternal mortality rate consistently have one thing in common: routine check-ins *at home*.

Let's take another look around the globe:

- In Denmark, a midwife will call the day after you leave the hospital, and then an at-home health visitor will come to the house within four to five days.
- In the Netherlands and Belgium, new mothers will have a *kraamverzorgster*, a maternity nurse who comes to the home to provide a minimum of twenty-four hours of care within the first eight days after discharge.

- For Swedish mothers, breastfeeding counseling is covered by insurance, and midwives conduct as many home visits as needed within the first four days after delivery (with more visits available if needed).
- France offers in-home postpartum care, *and* all birthing parents automatically receive a referral for pelvic floor therapy.

Oof that last one hits home for me. The irony is that the US doesn't even treat birth like other standard medical events. For example, my mom went through two knee replacements. Each time she had to stay one to two nights in the hospital and three to six weeks at home with a specific rehabilitation timeline, and completed a rigorous course of physical therapy for months.

Other countries don't necessarily have this one figured out yet; it seems we all struggle with maternal mental health. Stigma is often a substantial barrier when asking for help, which is wild to me because depression during pregnancy or the first year postpartum in the United States is twice as common as gestational diabetes. And perinatal mood and anxiety disorders are the number one medical complication related to childbearing.

This, of course, loops back to educating our healthcare providers and training them in maternal mental health so they can properly diagnose and provide treatment.

NEW PARENTS' RIGHTS

Did you know . . .

- UNICEF conducted research and found that compared to forty other developed countries, the United States ranked last in family-friendly policies.
- The US is the only developed country without any federal parental leave policy to protect workers when they welcome a new child.
- Only 14 percent of American workers have access to paid family leave.
- Forty percent of Americans *do not qualify* for the Family and Medical Leave Act.
- One in four women return to work just ten days after giving birth.

This all makes me sick. Parental leave has become very political recently, but the facts stand true: leave is instrumental in creating positive maternal and infant outcomes. For those giving birth, it allows time for physical recovery, emotional bonding, and better rates of breastfeeding success (which, in turn, decreases maternal and infant death rates). Partners can be caregivers to the birthing parent and the baby, which benefits the entire family.

In postpartum-positive countries, the amount of parental leave ranges—from weeks to months to even a year—but what differs from the US is that theirs is national law.

Finland is among the global leaders in parental leave in terms of sheer amount of time parents are entitled to take off upon having a child. Each parent gets a quota of 160 paid days off. This means the total length of parental leave is more than fourteen months, which can be taken across several periods until the child turns two. In Estonia, parents have a shared parental leave benefit of 475 calendar days, which takes into account the need for childcare.

Meanwhile, what are our lawmakers busy with in the US? A few days before writing this, I stumbled on an article that "Central New Jersey" will now be an officially recognized region, separate from the north and south regions, thanks to a new law passed by the state government. Gag me. *This* is what our elected officials are focused on while in office? Creating policies and enacting laws to ensure those who claim to live in Central New Jersey aren't ridiculed by people who refuse to believe it exists? What the F?

This leads to my next point: the role media (can) play in normalizing the transition into parenthood and shining a light on postpartum stories.

With a background in public relations and a history of working with media on news and lifestyle stories, I am over the moon that maternal mental health is getting more attention in mainstream media, even if a bulk of it stems from tragedy. In the past year, I've seen mainstream news stories about loss at the hands of postpartum depression, postpartum psychosis, and birth complications that shared the stories of those families impacted, shone a light on these mental health issues, and reinforced resources available to help new parents experiencing PMADs.

These articles, while incredibly difficult to read at times, help continue the conversation and help destigmatize maternal mental health—sharing the tragic ways PMADs can affect families when we don't properly support new parents or offer resources to help with their symptoms. We need to do more to add prevention efforts to this conversation. Postpartum Support International is an organization that is trying to extend their knowledge and passion by connecting with journalists for editorial opportunities—especially during Maternal Mental Health Month, which is honored in May each year.

If you have friends or family members who either chose not to have kids or are past the childbearing stage of their lives, they can still support this cause. In society we advocate and create policies and change to help pave the way for generations after us to have a safer and more supported experience.

I encourage you to raise your hand and get involved! Check out some of the amazing organizations that are working toward real change *now*.

WAYS TO GET INVOLVED

Policy Center for Maternal Mental Health

This organization is working to prevent the suffering of mothers, babies, and families associated with untreated maternal mental health disorders, like postpartum depression. They have driven the national conversation from one centered around raising awareness of one disorder, postpartum depression, to building a movement to address maternal mental health. The organization's work centers around closing gaps in the healthcare system by scaling change through identification of evidence-based and emerging solutions, cross-sector collaboration, and driving state and federal legislative and regulatory policy solutions.

The federal bill that the Policy Center for Maternal Mental Health championed was passed by Congress on December 23, 2022, and calls for the development of a national strategic plan to address maternal mental health. This will create the first ever national Maternal Mental Health task force. The bipartisan bill was introduced to create a national strategy to address maternal mental health disorders and coordination and integration of maternal mental health into existing maternal, infant, and mental health activities at the federal level.

More specifically, TRIUMPH promotes federal collaboration between agencies and departments to protect and address the mental health of new mothers and creates recommendations to state governors, House and Senate Committees, and relevant federal agencies to improve maternal mental health outcomes.

To get involved, visit 2020mom.org.

Postpartum Support International—Mind the Gap Coalition

Undiagnosed and untreated perinatal mental health disorders are a silent health crisis in the United States, deserving national recognition and action to save lives and improve the health and well-being of America's mothers, babies, fathers, families, and the community. Postpartum Support International works with a coalition of women, families, and leading organizations that have set forth a national strategic action plan to turn the tide in this crisis.

Together they stand for increasing research and funding and improving awareness and access to prevention, education, screening, diagnosis, treatment, and support services for pregnant and postpartum women and their families.

Their five critical areas are:

1. **Awareness and Help.** Raise public awareness of perinatal mental health, including greater understanding of the importance of prevention, recognition, and treatment, and how to seek help and support for mothers and families.

2. **Screening and Follow-up Care.** Ensure perinatal mental health screening is universal, standard, and routinely provided as part of healthcare delivery. Also, ensure that a positive screening includes follow-up diagnosis, referral, and access to treatment, during both pregnancy and postpartum, across all healthcare sectors.

3. **Access and Coverage.** Improve public and private access to and coverage of comprehensive prevention and integrated perinatal mental healthcare and treatment.

4. **Education & Training.** Provide perinatal mental health training for mental health and healthcare professionals, including education on screening, referral, treatment, and support services for mothers and families.

5. **Clinical & Prevention Research.** Support and promote population-based research and evidence-based prevention interventions that are culturally relevant to and inclusive of underserved populations and communities.

To get involved, visit postpartum.net.

Moms First

In March 2021, The Marshall Plan for Moms was introduced in the Senate. Endorsed by Girls Who Code, the National Partnership for Women and Families, MomsRising, the Women's March, the National Women's Law Center, the National Domestic Workers Alliance, the National Asian Pacific American Women's Forum, and the American Association of University Women, the bill calls for:

1. A robust paid leave plan, which is essential to securing the physical health and financial health of families, including emergency paid leave policies that would create a path toward permanent paid leave solutions.
2. Funding to rebuild and stabilize the childcare industry, which is essential to economic recovery and bolstering women in the labor force.
3. Major investments in education systems, providing funding to support and protect the safety and health of educators, support staff, students, and families.
4. Recurring child benefits and expanded and improved child tax credit and earned income tax credit to help reduce child poverty and provide economic security for families.
5. An expanded unemployment insurance program that benefits struggling workers, including those experiencing long-term unemployment.
6. Access to mental health support for mothers, which is essential to maintaining the health of the family.

To get involved, visit momsfirst.us.

Embrace uncertainty. Some of the most beautiful chapters in our lives won't have a title until much later.
—Bob Goff

I REMEMBER SAYING it so clearly and with total confidence. The day after giving birth, as I was drained emotionally, physically, and mentally, I looked at Kyle, pointed to our newborn baby girl, and said, "This is it—she's going to be an only child."

In that moment, I was serious. We had always had the idea in our heads to have multiple children. But after going through the traumatic birth and anxiety of the previous forty-eight hours, I was convinced I'd never go through with it again. I'd never allow myself to go through it again. And that was before experiencing postpartum depression and the pain that led to pelvic floor therapy. One and done.

Now, at 163 weeks postpartum, I'm pregnant again.

Expanding our family wasn't a decision I took lightly. In fact, I delayed our initial plan by six months because I didn't feel ready. I had a very conflicted mindset about the idea of having another baby. I talked to my therapist Lindsey about it (obviously), and we worked through some of my biggest fears: that I wasn't taking away anything from my daughter, I was adding a sibling to her life. I had a lot of guilt about the idea that I would be depriving my daughter of something. After all, my attention would always be split. I likely won't be able to hold them both while they are sick or be there for every single game, musical, or performance. I can only be in one place at one time. So, I had to keep telling myself I was going to do my best. Be the best version of me for them.

And I wanted more than anything to feel excited and not riddled with anxiety about going into round two. After all, this time I had a slight inkling as to what to truly expect. Not like those cute, naïve new parents going in for the first time. (No offense.)

It took a bit longer to conceive this time around. It's fascinating to me, those first few months when you are sad with disappointment seeing a spot of red. That's how I knew deep down I was ready to try and do it all over again. Finding out was a bit surreal this time. Nothing like my first. Leading up to it, I was more irritable than usual, more emotional, and had barely any PMS cramps. I was late, and then I was two days late and three days late. I knew why. I took the test, and while it was, of course, supposed to be fast —it was a rapid test—I swear that thing turned positive in an instant.

Kyle wasn't with me when I found out. I was away on business and away from my role as mommy—or so I thought. But Kyle was flying out to join me the following day for a quick two-day getaway—the first time it was just us for more than one night since our daughter was born.

I felt a lot of feelings in those first ten minutes after

seeing the test. Relieved that it happened, for one, being in the "trying" phase sucked. My life was unfolding in two-week phases: hoping to be pregnant, then finding out I wasn't. Waiting until I ovulated, and then hoping to be pregnant again, and then finding out I wasn't. I have the deepest empathy for those who struggle with infertility.

I was also a little sad, if I am honest. The phase of our life of just being the three of us is now dwindling. I won't be able to give my daughter my undivided attention; she'll have to share both of us. I was excited about growing our family, envisioning future holidays and celebrations with a new little one in the mix. And I was anxious—very anxious. My intrusive thoughts immediately started rushing in. I even had to give myself a pep talk in the hotel bathroom mirror. "You can do this. You are a great mom. You can get through it again."

A rapid-fire round of questions came charging into my mind:

- Am I happy? Of course.
- Am I scared? Oh, 100 percent.
- Do I want to go through the birthing process again? Nope.
- Do I know the pain is temporary? Yes, but that doesn't help in the moment!
- Am I worried I'll experience PPD again? Yes, the odds are likely.
- Do I feel supported and loved by my family and friends? Yes, even more so than last time.
- Am I going to do things differently this time? I hope so.
- Am I already stressed about childcare and finances? Sure am.

- Do I look at my sweet daughter and see her as the best big sister ever? Oh, with my whole heart.

It's challenging to not compare the two experiences, even now at this very early stage. Bringing my daughter into the world was an experience unlike any other, and in that sense, I know no other way. My anxiety keeps creeping in—what if it's the same? What if it's worse? I know that much of what will happen is outside of my control. Much of the experience of being a mother is outside of my control. How will I protect them? How will I raise them to be good, kind, and strong humans, and how will I one day let them go—fly free? I guess the saying, "Life is about the journey, not the destination," is on point. Life is so precious.

I started writing as a form of therapy for myself. To capture my thoughts to hold onto forever—maybe even share with my daughter should she choose to have a child one day. A small mental snapshot into a time of my life with so much change, fear, and absolute joy. I've always said that I believe everything in life happens for a reason. I had postpartum depression for a reason. I started writing for a reason. Now I guess we wait and see what the next chapter in life brings. My story is still a work in progress, but for now, pencils down.

ADDITIONAL RESOURCES

THERE IS a plethora of helpful information available to you—more than what I touched upon in this book. Every situation is unique, and you may have experiences when it comes to pregnancy, birth, and postpartum that I did not personally have. I've outlined some additional resources below that I touched upon throughout the book. Friendly reminder to always check that the resource you dive into is credible. Blogs and parenting advice articles are great for subjective advice, but you want to ensure you have accurate facts as well!

Truth #1: Time Doesn't Follow the Rules When You're Pregnant (or a New Mom)

- What to Expect app
- American Pregnancy Association (americanpregnancy.org)
- "Stages of Labor and Birth: Baby, It's Time!" (MayoClinic.org)

Truth #2: You Are Not in the Driver's Seat

- *The Birth Hour* podcast
- *Arrival Stories* by Amy Schumer and Christy Turlington Burns
- EvidenceBasedBirth.com
- *Ina May's Guide to Childbirth* by Ina May Gaskin
- *HypnoBirthing* by Marie Mongan, M. Ed., M. Hy
- "Types of Delivery: Childbirth Options, Differences and Benefits" (my.ClevelandClinic.org)
- "Questions to Ask on a Hospital Tour for Birth" (verywellfamily.com)
- "Labor Induction" (mayoclinic.org)
- "The 'Golden Hour': Giving Your Newborn the Best Start" (news.sanfordhealth.org)
- *Welcome to Fatherhood* by David Arrell
- *Baby Talk with Katie and David* podcast

Truth #3: Therapy Has a Place in Your Pregnancy Toolkit

- "Stigma, Prejudice and Discrimination Against People with Mental Illness" (psychiatry.org)
- PsychologyToday.com
- *Living Life Unconsciously* by Lindsey Ziegler, MA, LPC
- "The Pandemic Accelerant: How COVID-19 Advanced Our Mental Health Priorities" (un.org)
- Postpartum Support International (postpartum.net)
- "Patient Screening" (ACOG.org)

Truth #4: You'll Be in a "Postpartum Period" for the Rest of
Your Life

- "Physiology, Postpartum Changes"
  (ncbi.nlm.nih.gov)
- *The Fourth Trimester* by Kimberly Ann Johnson
- "What to Expect at a Postpartum Checkup—And
  Why the Visit Matters" (ACOG.org)
- American College of Obstetrics and Gynecology
  (ACOG.org)
- "Social Support Needs of First-Time Parents in the
  Early-Postpartum Period: A Qualitative Study"
  (ncbi.nlm.nih.gov)
- *Not Your Mother's Postpartum Book* by Caitlin
  Slavens and Chelsea Bodie

Truth #5: You'll Miss the "Old You," and That's Okay

- "I Love My Baby, but I Miss Myself" (mother.ly)
- "Alexandra Sacks: A New Way to Think About the
  Transition to Motherhood" TED talk
- "Flamingos and Mommas: Getting Our Pink Back"
  (medium.com)

Truth #6: You Might Have Some Really Dark Days

- *I Am One* Podcast
- Postpartum Support International
  (postpartum.net)
- 988Lifeline.org
- Pixels Journaling: Mood Track app

Truth #7: Your Heart will Leap for Joy, if not Initially, then Eventually

- "Bonding with Your Newborn: What to Know if You Don't Feel Connected Right Away" (ACOG.org)
- "I Didn't Bond with My Baby Right Away" (nytimes.com)
- "The Parent-Baby Bond: What if It Doesn't Happen Right Away?" (WhatToExpect.com)

Truth #8: You Can't 100 Percent Prepare for Motherhood

- "Female Infertility" (MayoClinic.org)
- "Male Infertility" (MayoClinic.org)
- Fertility Out Loud (FertilityOutLoud.com)
- "Finding Emotional Support After Pregnancy Loss" (ACOG.org)
- Pregnancy Loss Support Program (PregnancyLoss.org)
- Project NICU social media

Truth #9: Breastfeeding Isn't Natural, It's Learned

- "Breastfeeding" (WHO.int)
- "Infant Formula: Safety Do's and Don'ts" (FDA.gov)
- "Lactation Consultant" (AmericanPregnancy.org)
- "Barriers to Breastfeeding in the United States" (ncbi.nlm.nih.gov)
- American Academy of Pediatrics (AAP.org)
- "Key Breastfeeding Indicators" (CDC.gov)
- Chocolate Milk Café (ChocolateMilkCafe.org)

Truth #10: Work Every Day to Embrace Your New Body

- "Pregnancy Weight Gain: What's Healthy?" (MayoClinic.org)
- "Make Room for Baby" (MSIChicago.org)
- "Relaxin" (YourHomones.info)
- "Low Libido Postpartum" (WhatToExpect.com)
- "Vaginal Tears During Childbirth" (my.ClevelandClinic.org)
- "Episiotomy: When It's Needed, When It's Not" (MayoClinic.org)
- "The New Mother: Taking Care of Yourself After Birth" (StandfordChildrens.org)
- "How to Ease into a Postpartum Exercise Routine after Birth" (Parents.com)

Truth #11: I Never Truly Appreciated My Mother Until I Became One

- "Stay-at-Home Mothers Through the Years" (BLS.gov)
- "Almost 1 in 5 Stay-at-Home Parents in the U.S. Are Dads" (PewResearch.org)
- "How Much is a Mom Really Worth? The Amount May Surprise You." (Salary.com)
- "Postpartum Doula" (AmericanPregnancy.org)
- "5 Reasons Why You Need a Postpartum Support Network" (ACOG.org)

Truth #12: Renew Your Vows (if Marriage Is Your Cup of Tea)

- "When Couples Become Parents: The Impact on Your Relationship" (PsychologyToday.com)
- "The Magic Relationship Ratio, According to Science" (Gottman.com)
- *Babyproofing Your Marriage* by Stacie Cockrell, Cathy O'Neill, and Julia Stone
- *The Postpartum Partner* by Karen Kleiman
- *We're Pregnant: The First-Time Dad's Pregnancy Handbook* by Adrian Kulp
- *Dude, You're Gonna Be a Dad!* by John Pfeiffer

Truth #13: It's Not Cliché to Trust Your Instincts

- "New Study: Information Overload for Parents" (PyschologyToday.com)
- Big Little Feelings social media
- Momwell social media
- Psyched Mommy social media
- Hey, Sleepy Baby social media
- Taking Cara Babies social media
- *How to Have Your Second Child First* by Kerry Colburn and Rob Sorensen
- *Raising Good Humans* podcast

Truth #14: The "Fifth Trimester" Is Real

- *The Fifth Trimester* by Lauren Smith Brody (and on Social Media)
- "8 Facts about American Dads" (PewResearch.org)
- "How to Hire a Nanny" (WhatToExpect.com)

- "Day Care 101: How to Choose the Best Day Care Facility for Your Family" (WhatToExpect.com)
- "In the Absence of 'the Village,' Mothers Struggle Most" (Mother.ly)
- Moms First (MomsFirst.us)
- Next Chapter Careers (beccacarnahan.com)

Truth #15: You Have an Important Role Now

- "Growing Your Village: A Guide for New Parents" (Postpartum.net)
- *The Five Love Languages* by Gary Chapman
- "8 Ways Parents Say You Can Help After Baby Arrives" (Care.com)

Truth #16: The United States Needs to Level Up Postpartum Care

- "America Has the Highest Maternal Mortality Rate among Developed Nations" (Fortune.com)
- "International Labour Standards on Maternity Protection" (ILO.org)
- "What Does Postpartum Care Look like around the World?" (MavenClinic.com)
- "Impact of Doulas on Healthy Birth Outcomes" (ncbi.nlm.nih.gov)
- Postpartum Support International (Postpartum.net)
- Policy Center for Maternal Mental Health (2020Mom.org)
- Moms First (MomsFirst.us)

A Lie: Never Again

- "Are You Ready for Another One?" (BabyCenter.com)
- "Secondary Infertility" (My.ClevelandClinic.org)
- "How to Adjust to Having a Second Child" (PyschologyToday.com)
- *The Second Baby Book* by Sarah Ockwell-Smith

ACKNOWLEDGMENTS
WHERE TO BEGIN?

Thank you to my teachers and professors throughout my life who pushed me to write, creating a passion for writing and ultimately driving my career in communications.

Thank you to my parents and older brother for nurturing my creativity and personality at a young age, always advocating for me to use my voice.

Thank you to my husband, best friend and life partner – Kyle, for supporting me and loving me through it all.

Thank you to my therapist – Lindsey, for guiding me through my personal mental health journey.

Thank you to my mom tribe – Jenn, Julie, Karen, Kim, Stacey, and Rosie, who I can always rely on to keep it real. So grateful to be able to support each other as we raise the next generation of strong and kind humans.

Thank you, Google, for my endless searches on how to publish a book. It always had an answer. And to those published authors in my life who I reached out to for advice – Becca, Katie and Sam.

Thank you to the incredible professionals who helped me

make this book a reality. M.C. Calvi, who was the first person to ever read the full manuscript and provided incredible value and helped me through my developmental edit. Mickey Shu-Ting Chan and Dani Marcel, who created a beautiful cover that over exceeded my expectations, filled with symbolic touches. Lastly, Sara DeGonia, who helped get this manuscript over the finish line as copyeditor.

September 13, 2023
(Four weeks and two days)

Hi, tonight I found out there really is a "you." You are already so incredibly loved and you will have the most amazing big sister to grow up with and learn from. I hope you both always have each other's love and support. I'd be lying if I said I wasn't nervous or anxious. I'm only human. I'm your mom now and forever, and I can't wait to meet you! We will have incredible adventures together... just wait and see! Until then, stay safe and cozy. I love you.

- Love, Mom

ABOUT THE AUTHOR

Colleen Imler is a communications and public relations professional by day and an advocate for mental health by night. Around the clock she is a mom, wife, sister, daughter and friend. She stays grounded and relaxed by being around animals and nature. Kayaking out on a lake is her happy place.

She started volunteering with Postpartum Support International (PSI) in 2022 and served as a board member for the New Jersey chapter. Her passion for advocating for maternal mental health and navigating the postpartum experience stems from her own challenges transitioning into motherhood. After welcoming her daughter amid a global pandemic during the summer of 2020, she experienced postpartum depression and immediately sought out help.

Today she lives in New Jersey with her husband, daughter, beloved dog, and second child on the way!